아서와
도둑맞은 자전거의
미스터리

CONTENTS

대한민국 영어 학습자라면 꼭 한번 읽어봐야 할, 아서 챕터북 시리즈!

아서 챕터북 시리즈(Arthur Chapter Book series)는 미국의 작가 마크 브라운(Marc Brown)이 쓴 책입니다. 레이크우드 초등학교에 다니는 주인공 아서(Arthur)가 소소한 일상에서 벌이는 다양한 에피소드를 담은 이 책은, 기본적으로 미국 초등학생들을 위해 쓰인 책이지만 누구나 공감할 만한 재미있는 스토리로 출간된 지 30년이 넘은 지금까지 남녀노소 모두에게 큰 사랑을 받고 있습니다. 아서가 주인공으로 등장하는 이야기는 리더스북과 챕터북 등 다양한 형태로 출판되었는데, 현재 미국에서만 누적 판매 부수가 6천6백만 부를 돌파한 상황으로 대한민국 인구 숫자보다 더 많은 책이 판매된 것을 생각하면 그 인기가 어느 정도 인지 실감할 수 있습니다.

특히 이『아서 챕터북』은 한국에서 영어 학습자를 위한 최적의 원서로 큰 사랑을 받고 있기도 합니다. 『영어 낭독 훈련』, 『잠수네 영어 학습법』, 『솔빛이네 엄마표 영어연수』 등 많은 영어 학습법 책들에서『아서 챕터북』을 추천 도서로 선정하고 있으며, 수많은 영어 고수들과 영어 선생님들, '엄마표 영어'를 진행하는 부모님들에게도 반드시 거쳐 가야 하는 영어원서로 전폭적인 지지를 얻고 있습니다.

번역과 단어장이 포함된 워크북, 그리고 오디오북까지 담긴 풀 패키지!

이 책은 이렇게 큰 사랑을 받고 있는 영어원서『아서 챕터북』시리즈에, 더욱 탁월한 학습 효과를 거둘 수 있도록 다양한 콘텐츠를 덧붙인 책입니다.

- 영어원서: 본문에 나온 어려운 어휘에 볼드 처리가 되어 있어 단어를 더욱 분명히 인지하며 자연스럽게 암기하게 됩니다.
- 단어장: 원서에 나온 어려운 어휘가 '한영'은 물론 '영영' 의미까지 완벽하게 정리되어 있으며, 반복되는 단어까지 넣어두어 자연스럽게 복습이 되도록 구성했습니다.
- 번역: 영어와 비교할 수 있도록 직역에 가까운 번역을 담았습니다. 원서 읽기에 익숙하지 않는 초보 학습자들도 어려움 없이 내용을 파악할 수 있습니다.
- 퀴즈: 현직 원어민 교사가 만든 이해력 점검 퀴즈가 들어있습니다.
- 오디오북: 미국 현지에서 판매중인 빠른 속도의 오디오북(분당 약 145단어)과

국내에서 녹음된 따라 읽기용 오디오북(분당 약 110단어)을 포함하고 있어 듣기 훈련은 물론 소리 내어 읽기에까지 폭넓게 사용할 수 있습니다.

이 책의 수준과 타깃 독자

- 미국 원어민 기준: 유치원 ~ 초등학교 저학년
- 한국 학습자 기준: 초등학교 저학년 ~ 중학교 1학년
- 영어원서 완독 경험이 없는 초보 영어 학습자 (토익 기준 450~750점대)
- 비슷한 수준의 다른 챕터북: Magic Tree House, Marvin Redpost, Zack Files, Captain Underpants
- 도서 분량: 5,000단어 초반 (약 5,000~5,200단어)

아서 챕터북, 이렇게 읽어보세요!

- **단어 암기는 이렇게!** 처음 리딩을 시작하기 전, 해당 챕터에 나오는 단어들을 눈으로 쭉 훑어봅니다. 모르는 단어는 좀 더 주의 깊게 보되, 손으로 써가면서 완벽하게 암기할 필요는 없습니다. 본문을 읽으면서 이 단어들을 다시 만나게 되는데, 그 과정에서 단어의 쓰임새와 어감을 자연스럽게 익히게 됩니다. 이렇게 책을 읽은 후에, 단어를 다시 한번 복습하세요. 복습할 때는 중요하다고 생각하는 단어들을 손으로 써가면서 꼼꼼하게 외우는 것도 좋습니다. 이런 방식으로 책을 읽다보면, 많은 단어를 빠르고 부담 없이 익히게 됩니다.

- **리딩할 때는 리딩에만 집중하자!** 원서를 읽는 중간 중간 모르는 단어가 나온다고 워크북을 들춰보거나, 곧바로 번역을 찾아보는 것은 매우 좋지 않은 습관입니다. 모르는 단어나 이해가 가지 않는 문장이 나온다고 해도 펜으로 가볍게 표시만 해두고, 전체적인 맥락을 잡아가며 빠르게 읽어나가세요. 리딩을 할 때는 속도에 대한 긴장감을 잃지 않으면서 리딩에만 집중하는 것이 좋습니다. 모르는 단어와 문장은, 리딩이 끝난 후에 한꺼번에 정리해보는 '리뷰'시간을 갖습니다. 리뷰를 할 때는 번역은 물론 단어장과 사전도 꼼꼼하게 확인하면서 왜 이해가 되지 않았는지 확인해 봅니다.

- **번역 활용은 이렇게!** 이해가 가지 않는 문장은 번역을 통해서 그 의미를 파악할

수 있습니다. 하지만 한국어와 영어는 정확히 1:1 대응이 되지 않기 때문에 번역을 활용하는 데에도 지혜가 필요합니다. 의역이 된 부분까지 억지로 의미를 대응해서 암기하려고 하기보다, 어떻게 그런 의미가 만들어진 것인지 추측하면서 번역은 참고자료로 활용하는 것이 좋습니다.

- **듣기 훈련은 이렇게!** 리스닝 실력을 향상시키길 원한다면 오디오북을 적극적으로 활용하세요. 처음에는 오디오북을 틀어놓고 눈으로 해당 내용을 따라 읽으면서 훈련을 하고, 이것이 익숙해지면 오디오북만 틀어놓고 '귀를 통해' 책을 읽어보세요. 눈으로는 한 번도 읽지 않은 책을 귀를 통해 완벽하게 이해할 수 있다면 이후에는 영어 듣기로 고생하는 일은 거의 없을 것입니다.

- **소리 내어 읽고 녹음하자!** 이 책은 특히 소리 내어 읽기(Voice Reading)에 최적화된 문장 길이와 구조를 가지고 있습니다. 또한 오디오북 CD에 포함된 '따라 읽기용' 오디오북으로 소리 내어 읽기 훈련을 함께할 수 있습니다. 소리 내어 읽기를 하면서 내가 읽은 것을 녹음하고 들어보세요! 자신의 영어 발음을 들어보는 것은 몹시 민망한 일이지만, 그 과정을 통해서 의식적·무의식적으로 발음을 교정하게 됩니다. 이렇게 영어로 소리를 만들어 본 경험은 이후 탄탄한 스피킹 실력의 밑거름이 될 것입니다.

- **2~3번 반복해서 읽자!** 영어 초보자라면 2~3회 반복해서 읽을 것을 추천합니다. 초보자일수록 처음 읽을 때는 생소한 단어들과 스토리 때문에 내용 파악에 급급할 수밖에 없습니다. 하지만 일단 내용을 파악한 후에 다시 읽으면 어휘와 문장 구조 등 다른 부분까지 관찰하면서 조금 더 깊이 있게 읽을 수 있고, 그 과정에서 리딩 속도도 빨라지고 리딩 실력을 더 확고하게 다지게 됩니다.

- **'시리즈'로 꾸준히 읽자!** 한 작가의 책을 시리즈로 읽는 것 또한 영어 실력 향상에 큰 도움이 됩니다. 같은 등장인물이 다시 나오기 때문에 내용 파악이 더 수월할 뿐 아니라, 작가가 사용하는 어휘와 표현들도 자연스럽게 반복되기 때문에 탁월한 복습 효과까지 얻을 수 있습니다. 『아서 챕터북』 시리즈는 현재 10권, 총 50,000단어 분량이 출간되어 있습니다. 이 책들을 시리즈로 꾸준히 읽으면서 영어 실력을 쑥쑥 향상시켜 보세요!

영어원서 본문 구성

원어민이 읽는 일반 원서와 같은 텍스트지만, 암기해야 할 중요 어휘들은 볼드체로 표시되어 있습니다. 이 어휘들은 지금 들고 계신 워크북에 챕터별로 정리되어 있습니다.

학습 심리학 연구 결과에 따르면, 한 단어씩 따로 외우는 단어 암기는 거의 효과가 없다고 합니다. 대신 단어를 제대로 외우기 위해서는 문맥(Context) 속에서 단어를 암기해야 하며, 한 단어 당 문맥 속에서 15번 이상 마주칠 때 완벽하게 암기할 수 있다고 합니다.

이 책의 본문은 중요 어휘를 볼드로 강조하여, 문맥 속의 단어들을 더 확실히 인지(Word Cognition in Context)하도록 돕고 있습니다. 또한 대부분의 중요한 단어들은 다른 챕터에서도 반복해서 등장하기 때문에 이 책을 읽는 것만으로도 자연스럽게 어휘력을 향상시킬 수 있습니다.

또한 본문에는 내용 이해를 돕기 위해 '각주'가 첨가되어 있습니다. 각주는 굳이 암기할 필요는 없지만, 알아두면 내용을 더 깊이 있게 이해할 수 있어 원서를 읽는 재미가 배가됩니다.

워크북(Workbook)의 구성

Check Your Reading Speed
해당 챕터의 단어 수가 기록되어 있어, 리딩 속도를 측정할 수 있습니다. 특히 리딩 속도를 중시하는 독자들이 유용하게 사용할 수 있습니다.

Build Your Vocabulary
본문에 볼드 표시되어 있는 단어들이 정리되어 있습니다. 리딩 전, 후에 반복해서 보면 원서를 더욱 쉽게 읽을 수 있고, 어휘력도 빠르게 향상됩니다.

단어는 〈빈도 – 스펠링 – 발음기호 – 품사 – 한글 뜻 – 영문 뜻〉 순서로 표기되어 있으며 빈도 표시(★)가 많을수록 필수 어휘입니다. 반복 등장하는 단어는 빈도 대신 '복습'으로 표기되어 있습니다. 품사는 아래와 같이 표기했습니다.

n. 명사 ｜ a. 형용사 ｜ ad. 부사 ｜ v. 동사
conj. 접속사 ｜ prep. 전치사 ｜ int. 감탄사 ｜ idiom 숙어 및 관용구

Comprehension Quiz
간단한 퀴즈를 통해 읽은 내용에 대한 이해력을 점검해 볼 수 있습니다.

번역
영문과 비교할 수 있도록 최대한 직역에 가까운 번역을 담았습니다.

오디오북 CD 구성

이 책은 '듣기 훈련'과 '소리 내어 읽기 훈련'을
위한 2가지 종류의 오디오북이 포함되어 있습
니다.

- 듣기 훈련용 오디오북: 분당 145단어 속도
  (미국 현지 판매 중인 오디오북)
- 소리 내어 읽기 훈련용 오디오북: 분당 110
  단어 속도

오디오북은 MP3 파일로 제공되는 MP3 기기나
컴퓨터에 옮겨서 사용하셔야 합니다. 오디오북
에 이상이 있을 경우 helper@longtailbooks.co.kr로 메일을 주시면 자세한 안내를
받으실 수 있습니다.

EBS 동영상 강의 안내

EBS의 어학사이트(EBSlang.co.kr)에서 『아서 챕터북』 동영상 강의가 진행되고 있습니다.
영어 어순의 원리에 맞게 빠르고 정확하게 이해하는 법을 완벽하게 코치해주는 국내 유일의 강의!
저렴한 수강료에 완강 시 50% 환급까지!
지금 바로 열광적인 수강 평가와 샘플 강의를 확인하세요!

http://www.EBSreading.com

Chapter 1

1. What was Francine doing with her family?

    A. She was working on her homework.

    B. She was just sitting in her chair.

    C. She was watching TV.

    D. She was cooking dinner.

2. Why was Francine sulking?

    A. She wanted to eat something else.

    B. She wanted her dad to fix her bike.

    C. She wanted a new car.

    D. She wanted a new bike.

3. **What did Francine say would happen to her without a bike?**

   A. She would just die.

   B. She would be late to school.

   C. She would lose all of her friends.

   D. She would ruin her shoes by walking everywhere.

4. **Which of the following does NOT describe the bike that Francine received from her father?**

   A. It had been used by her father when he was Francine's age.

   B. It was bright purple with chipped paint.

   C. It had been in the basement.

   D. It had twenty-one gears.

5. **How did Francine react to her father giving her the bike?**

   A. She had hope that she could fix it up.

   B. She was excited to finally have her own bike.

   C. She was disappointed that it was old and ugly.

   D. She was grateful that her father was so generous.

1분에 몇 단어를 읽는지 리딩 속도를 측정해보세요.

$$\frac{521 \ words}{reading \ time \ (\quad) \ sec} \times 60 = (\quad) \ WPM$$

Build Your Vocabulary

fold [fould] v. (두 손·팔 등을) 끼다; 접다; 감싸다; n. 주름; 접는 부분
If you fold your arms or hands, you bring them together and cross or link them, for example over your chest.

sulk [sʌlk] v. 부루퉁하다, 샐쭉하다; n. 부루퉁함
If you sulk, you are silent and bad-tempered for a while because you are annoyed about something.

out of sorts idiom 몸이 편치 않다; 의기소침하다
If you are out of sorts, you feel slightly unwell, ill, or bad-tempered.

bit [bit] n. 조금, 약간; 한 조각
A bit means to a small extent or degree. It is sometimes used to make a statement less extreme.

get one's way idiom 바라던 것을 얻다, 생각대로 하다, 제멋대로 하다
If someone gets their way, no one stops them doing what they want to do.

afford [əfɔ́:rd] v. ~을 할 여유가 되다; 제공하다
If you cannot afford something, you do not have enough money to pay for it.

fair [fɛər] a. 공정한; 타당한; 아름다운; n. 박람회
Something or someone that is fair is reasonable, right, and just.

gasp [gæsp] v. 숨이 턱 막히다, 헉 하고 숨을 쉬다; n. 헉 하는 소리를 냄
When you gasp, you take a short quick breath through your mouth, especially when you are surprised, shocked, or in pain.

drop [drap] v. 떨어뜨리다; 약해지다, 낮추다; (사람·짐을) 내리다; n. 방울; 하락, 감소
If a person or a part of their body drops to a lower position, or if they drop a part of their body to a lower position, they move to that position, often in a tired and lifeless way.

knee [niː] n. 무릎
Your knee is the place where your leg bends.

grab [græb] v. 붙잡다, 움켜잡다; n. 와락 잡아채려고 함
If you grab something, you take it or pick it up suddenly and roughly.

give up idiom 그만두다; 단념하다; 포기하다
If you give something up, you stop trying to do it or having it.

giggle [gigl] v. 피식 웃다, 킥킥거리다; n. 피식 웃음, 킥킥거림
If someone giggles, they laugh in a childlike way, because they are amused, nervous, or embarrassed.

silly [síli] a. 우스꽝스러운, 유치한; 어리석은, 바보 같은; n. 바보
If you say that someone or something is silly, you mean that they are foolish, childish, or ridiculous.

trick [trik] n. 장난; 속임수; 묘기; v. 속이다, 속임수를 쓰다; a. 교묘한
A trick is something you do to surprise someone and to make other people laugh.

salute [səlúːt] v. 경례를 하다; 경의를 표하다, 절하다; n. 거수 경례; 인사, 절
If you salute someone, you greet them or show your respect with a formal sign.

work on idiom (원하는) 효과가 나다; (해결하기 위해) ~에 애쓰다
To work on someone means to try to persuade or influence them.

stroke [strouk] v. 쓰다듬다; n. 쓰다듬기; 타격, 치기

If you stroke someone or something, you move your hand slowly and gently over them.

chin [ʧin] n. 턱

Your chin is the part of your face that is below your mouth and above your neck.

come over idiom (어떤 기분이) 갑자기 들다; (특히 누구의 집에) 들르다

If a strong feeling comes over you, you suddenly experience it.

besides [bisáidz] ad. 게다가, 뿐만 아니라; prep. 외에

Besides is used to emphasize an additional point that you are making, especially one that you consider to be important.

basement [béismənt] n. (건물의) 지하층

The basement of a building is a floor built partly or completely below ground level.

storage [stɔ́:ridʒ] n. 저장, 보관; 저장고

If you refer to the storage of something, you mean that it is kept in a special place until it is needed.

compartment [kəmpá:rtmənt] n. (물건 보관용) 칸; (칸막이를 한) 객실

A compartment is one of the separate parts of an object that is used for keeping things in.

lock [lak] v. (자물쇠로) 잠그다; 고정시키다; n. 자물쇠 (**unlock** v. (열쇠로) 열다)

If you unlock something such as a door, a room, or a container that has a lock, you open it using a key.

bottom [bátəm] a. 맨 아래쪽에; n. 맨 아래; 뒷면; 바닥

The bottom thing or layer in a series of things or layers is the lowest one.

point [pɔint] n. 의미; 요점; v. (손가락 등으로) 가리키다; (길을) 알려 주다

If you ask what the point of something is, or say that there is no point in it, you are indicating that a particular action has no purpose or would not be useful.

cobweb [kábwèb] n. 거미줄
A cobweb is the net which a spider makes for catching insects.

aim [eim] v. 겨누다; 목표하다; 대상으로 하다; n. 겨냥, 조준; 목표
If you aim a weapon or object at something or someone, you point it toward them before firing or throwing it.

flashlight [flǽʃlàit] n. 손전등; 섬광
A flashlight is a small electric light which gets its power from batteries and which you can carry in your hand.

rummage [rʌ́midʒ] v. 뒤지다; n. 뒤지기
If you rummage through something, you search for something you want by moving things around in a careless or hurried way.

aside [əsáid] ad. 한쪽으로; (길을) 비켜; (나중에 쓰려고) 따로
If you move something aside, you move it to one side of you.

reveal [riví:l] v. (보이지 않던 것을) 드러내 보이다; (비밀 등을) 밝히다
If you reveal something that has been out of sight, you uncover it so that people can see it.

wheel [hwi:l] v. (바퀴 달린 것을) 밀다; 태우고 가다; n. 바퀴; (자동차 등의) 핸들
If you wheel an object that has wheels somewhere, you push it along.

one's face falls idiom 실망하다
If someone's face falls, they suddenly look very disappointed.

bright [brait] a. 선명한, 밝은; 눈부신, 빛나는; 똑똑한
A bright color is strong and noticeable, and not dark.

chip [ʧip] v. 이가 빠지다; 깎다; n. 감자 칩; 조각, 부스러기 (chipped a. 깨진)
If you chip something or if it chips, a small piece is broken off it.

rust [rʌst] v. 녹슬다, 부식하다; n. 녹
When a metal object rusts, it becomes covered in rust and often loses its strength.

handlebar [hǽndlbɑ:r] n. (pl.) (자전거 등의) 핸들
The handlebar of a bicycle consist of a curved metal bar with handles at each end which are used for steering.

glitter [glítər] n. 반짝반짝 하는 빛; 화려함; v. 반짝반짝 빛나다; (눈을) 번득이다 (glittery a. 반짝반짝 하는)
Something that is glittery shines with a lot of very small points of light.

burn [bə:rn] v. 태우다; (햇볕 등에) 타다; n. 화상 (burnt a. (불에) 탄)
If you burn something, you destroy or damage it with fire.

wipe [waip] v. (먼지·물기 등을) 닦다; 지우다; n. 닦기, 훔치기
If you wipe something, you rub its surface to remove dirt or liquid from it.

enormous [inɔ́:rməs] a. 막대한, 거대한
Something that is enormous is extremely large in size or amount.

inspect [inspékt] v. 점검하다, 검사하다; 사찰하다
If you inspect something, you look at every part of it carefully in order to find out about it or check that it is all right.

definite [défənit] a. 분명한, 뚜렷한; 확실한, 확고한 (definitely ad. 분명히, 틀림없이)
You use definitely to emphasize that something is the case, or to emphasize the strength of your intention or opinion.

collector [kəléktər] n. 수집가; 징수원
A collector is a person who collects things of a particular type as a hobby.

gear [giər] n. 기어; (특정 활동에 필요한) 장비, 복장
The gears on a machine or vehicle are a device for changing the rate at which energy is changed into motion.

confuse [kənfjú:z] v. (사람을) 혼란시키다; 혼동하다 (confusing a. 혼란스러운)
Something that is confusing makes it difficult for people to know exactly what is happening or what to do.

plenty [plénti] n. 풍부한 양; 풍요로움; ad. 많이; (~하기에) 충분히 큰
Plenty is used especially to indicate that there is enough of something, or more than you need.

click [klik] v. 딸깍 하는 소리를 내다; (마우스를) 클릭하다; n. 딸깍 하는 소리
If something clicks or if you click it, it makes a short, sharp sound.

spin [spin] v. (spun-spun) 돌리다, 회전시키다; (휙) 돌아서다; n. 회전, 돌기
If something spins or if you spin it, it turns quickly around a central point.

ride [raid] v. (rode-ridden) (차량·자전거·말 등을) 타다;
n. (차량·자전거 등을) 타고 달리기; 여정
When you ride a bicycle or a motorcycle, you sit on it, control it, and
travel along on it.

appreciate [əprí:ʃièit] v. 진가를 인정하다; 고마워하다
If you appreciate something, for example a piece of music or good food,
you like it because you recognize its good qualities.

pat [pæt] v. 쓰다듬다, 토닥거리다; n. 쓰다듬기
If you pat something or someone, you tap them lightly, usually with
your hand held flat.

sigh [sai] v. 한숨을 쉬다, 한숨짓다; n. 한숨; 탄식
When you sigh, you let out a deep breath, as a way of expressing feelings
such as disappointment, tiredness, or pleasure.

Chapter 2

1. **What did Muffy consider educational and important to watch on TV?**
   A. The Evening News
   B. The Weather Channel
   C. The Home Shopping Channel
   D. The Discovery Channel

2. **Why did Francine say that she had chosen her bike?**
   A. She said it was a family heirloom.
   B. She said that three gears were enough.
   C. She said that she liked the color purple.
   D. She said that she was saving money for something else.

3. **How did Buster make fun of Francine during class?**

   A. He said that she looked like a marshmallow.

   B. He said that ancient people built Francine's bike.

   C. He said that she was poor and had old things.

   D. He said that her bike was just trash.

4. **What did Muffy say to try to help Francine?**

   A. She said that she would buy Francine a new bike.

   B. She said that Francine should get rid of her old bike.

   C. She said that it wasn't Francine's fault that she had an old bike.

   D. She said that Francine's father really cared about Francine's bike.

5. **How did Francine feel when everyone in class got quiet?**

   A. She felt embarrassed.

   B. She felt angry.

   C. She felt confused.

   D. She felt grateful.

1분에 몇 단어를 읽는지 리딩 속도를 측정해보세요.

$$\frac{451 \text{ words}}{\text{reading time ( ) sec}} \times 60 = (\quad) \text{ WPM}$$

Build Your Vocabulary

admit [ædmít] v. 인정하다, 시인하다
If you admit that something bad, unpleasant, or embarrassing is true, you agree, often unwillingly, that it is true.

vehicle [víːikl] n. 차량, 탈것, 운송 수단
A vehicle is a machine such as a car, bus, or truck which has an engine and is used to carry people from place to place.

chase [ʧeis] v. 뒤쫓다, 추적하다; 추구하다; n. 추적; 추구함
If you chase someone, or chase after them, you run after them or follow them quickly in order to catch or reach them.

villain [vílən] n. 악당; 악인, 악한
A villain is someone who deliberately harms other people or breaks the law in order to get what he or she wants.

assorted [əsɔ́ːrtid] a. 여러 가지의, 갖은
A group of assorted things is a group of similar things that are of different sizes or colors or have different qualities.

lock [lak] v. (자물쇠로) 잠그다; 고정시키다; n. 자물쇠
(lock up idiom ~을 안전한 곳에 넣다)
If you lock up something, you put it in a place or container which you fasten with a lock.

educational [èdʒukéiʃənl] a. 교육의, 교육적인
An educational experience teaches you something.

channel [ʧǽnl] n. (텔레비전·라디오의) 채널; 경로, 수단; v. (돈·감정 등을) 쏟다
A channel is a television station.

attention [əténʃən] n. 주의, 주목; 관심 (**pay attention** idiom 주의를 기울이다)
If you pay attention to someone, you watch them, listen to them, or take notice of them.

fabulous [fǽbjuləs] a. 기막히게 좋은; 엄청난, 굉장한
If you describe something as fabulous, you are emphasizing that you like it a lot or think that it is very good.

opportunity [àpərtjúːnəti] n. 기회
An opportunity is a situation in which it is possible for you to do something that you want to do.

roll one's eyes idiom 눈을 굴리다
If you roll your eyes, you move them round and upward when you are frightened, bored, or annoyed.

take one's chance idiom ~을 운에 맡기고 해보다; ~의 기회를 이용하다
When you take your chance, you try to do something although there is a large risk of danger or failure.

ride [raid] v. (rode-ridden) (차량·자전거·말 등을) 타다;
n. (차량·자전거 등을) 타고 달리기; 여정
When you ride a bicycle or a motorcycle, you sit on it, control it, and travel along on it.

skip [skip] v. 건너뛰다, 생략하다; 깡충깡충 뛰다; n. 깡충깡충 뛰기
If you skip something that you usually do or something that most people do, you decide not to do it.

stare [stɛər] v. 빤히 쳐다보다, 응시하다; n. 빤히 쳐다보기, 응시
If you stare at someone or something, you look at them for a long time.

century [sénʧəri] n. 1세기, 100년
A century is a period of a hundred years that is used when stating a date.

latest [léitist] a. 최신의, 최근의
You can use latest to describe something that is very new and modern and is better than older things of a similar kind.

gear [giər] n. 기어; (특정 활동에 필요한) 장비, 복장
The gears on a machine or vehicle are a device for changing the rate at which energy is changed into motion.

alloy [ǽlɔi] n. 합금; v. 합금하다
An alloy is a metal that is made by mixing two or more types of metal together.

frame [freim] n. (가구·건물·차량 등의) 뼈대; 틀, 액자; v. 틀에 넣다; 죄를 뒤집어씌우다
The frame of an object such as a building, chair, or window is the arrangement of wooden, metal, or plastic bars between which other material is fitted, and which give the object its strength and shape.

radial [réidiəl] a. 방사상의; 반지름의
Radial refers to the pattern that you get when straight lines are drawn from the center of a circle to a number of points round the edge.

brake [breik] n. 브레이크, 제동 장치; 제동; v. 브레이크를 밟다; 속도를 줄이다
Brakes are devices in a vehicle that make it go slower or stop.

frown [fraun] v. 얼굴을 찌푸리다; n. 찡그림, 찌푸림
When someone frowns, their eyebrows become drawn together, because they are annoyed or puzzled.

tradition [trədíʃən] n. 전통
A tradition is a custom or belief that has existed for a long time.

heirloom [έərlùːm] n. (집안의) 가보
An heirloom is an ornament or other object that has belonged to a family for a very long time and that has been handed down from one generation to another.

trick [trik] n. 묘기; 속임수; 장난; v. 속이다, 속임수를 쓰다; a. 교묘한
A trick is a clever or skilful action that someone does in order to entertain people.

convince [kənvíns] v. 설득하다; 납득시키다, 확신시키다 (convinced a. 확신하는)
If you are convinced that something is true, you feel sure that it is true.

whisper [hwíspər] v. 속삭이다, 소곤거리다; n. 속삭임, 소곤거리는 소리
When you whisper, you say something very quietly.

wheel [hwi:l] n. 바퀴; (자동차 등의) 핸들; v. (바퀴 달린 것을) 밀다; 태우고 가다
The wheels of a vehicle are the circular objects which are fixed underneath it and which enable it to move along the ground.

invent [invént] v. 발명하다; (사실이 아닌 것을) 지어내다
If you invent something such as a machine or process, you are the first person to think of it or make it.

approximate [əpráksəmət] a. 대략의, 거의 정확한; v. 비슷하다
(approximately ad. 거의 정확하게, ~의 가까이)
An approximate number, time, or position is close to the correct number, time, or position, but is not exact.

mix up idiom ~을 (~와) 혼동하다
If you mix up someone or something, you mistake them for someone or something else.

sigh [sai] v. 한숨을 쉬다, 한숨짓다; n. 한숨; 탄식
When you sigh, you let out a deep breath, as a way of expressing feelings such as disappointment, tiredness, or pleasure.

confuse [kənfjú:z] v. (사람을) 혼란시키다; 혼동하다 (confusing a. 혼란스러운)
Something that is confusing makes it difficult for people to know exactly what is happening or what to do.

ancient [éinʃənt] a. 고대의; 아주 오래된; n. (pl.) 고대인
Ancient means belonging to the distant past, especially to the period in history before the end of the Roman Empire.

wave [weiv] v. 흔들다; 손짓하다; n. 파도, 물결; (팔·손·몸을) 흔들기
If you wave or wave your hand, you move your hand from side to side in the air, usually in order to say hello or goodbye to someone.

snicker [sníkər] v. 킬킬 웃다, 숨죽여 웃다; n. 킬킬 웃음, 숨죽여 웃는 웃음

If you snicker, you laugh quietly in a disrespectful way, for example at something rude or embarrassing.

pick on idiom ~을 괴롭히다; 비난하다; ~을 선택하다

If you pick on someone, you treat them badly or unfairly, especially repeatedly.

fault [fɔːlt] n. 잘못, 책임; 단점; 결함; v. 나무라다, 흠잡다

If a bad or undesirable situation is your fault, you caused it or are responsible for it.

go on idiom 말을 계속하다; (어떤 상황이) 계속되다; 시작하다

When you go on, you continue speaking after a short pause.

blink [bliŋk] v. 눈을 깜박이다; (불빛이) 깜박거리다; n. 눈을 깜박거림

When you blink or when you blink your eyes, you shut your eyes and very quickly open them again.

press [pres] v. 누르다; (무엇을 하도록) 입력을 가하다; n. 언론; 인쇄

If you press something somewhere, you push it firmly against something else.

chest [tʃest] ① n. 가슴, 흉부 ② n. 상자, 궤

Your chest is the top part of the front of your body where your ribs, lungs, and heart are.

embarrass [imbǽrəs] v. 당황스럽게 하다, 쑥스럽게 하다; 곤란하게 하다
(embarrassed a. 쑥스러운, 당황스러운)

A person who is embarrassed feels shy, ashamed, or guilty about something.

Chapter 3

1. **Where did Francine put the bike after school?**

   A. In the dumpster

   B. Inside her locker

   C. Next to the bike rack

   D. Behind a garbage can

2. **What did Buster want to say to Francine?**

   A. He wanted to say sorry.

   B. He wanted to ask for help with class.

   C. He wanted to insult her some more.

   D. He wanted to ask where she put her bike.

3. **What did Arthur say the bike was like?**
   A. He said the bike was like a piece of trash.
   B. He said the bike was like his father's old frying pan.
   C. He said the bike was like his mother's old raincoat.
   D. He said the bike was like a collector's item.

4. **Why did Francine say that she wasn't using her bike?**
   A. She had forgotten where she put it.
   B. She had a flat tire.
   C. She felt like walking.
   D. Someone had stolen it.

5. **Why did Francine not want to go with her friends to the Sugar Bowl?**
   A. She felt out of place.
   B. She wasn't feeling hungry.
   C. She didn't have a way to get there.
   D. She had chores to do at home.

1분에 몇 단어를 읽는지 리딩 속도를 측정해보세요.

$$\frac{485 \text{ words}}{\text{reading time (} \qquad \text{) sec}} \times 60 = (\qquad) \text{ WPM}$$

Build Your Vocabulary

✵ **rush** [rʌʃ] v. 급히 움직이다, 서두르다; 재촉하다; n. 혼잡, 분주함; (강한 감정이) 치밀어 오름
If you rush somewhere, you go there quickly.

✵ **hall** [hɔːl] n. (건물 안의) 복도; 현관; 넓은 방, 홀
A hall in a building is a long passage with doors into rooms on both sides of it.

✵ **mind** [maind] v. 상관하다, 개의하다; n. 마음, 정신; 신경, 관심
If you do not mind something, you are not annoyed or bothered by it.

stand out idiom 두드러지다, 눈에 띄다; 뛰어나다
If someone or something stands out, they are much better than other similar things or people.

✵ **tease** [tiːz] v. 놀리다, 장난하다; n. 장난, 놀림
To tease someone means to laugh at them or make jokes about them in order to embarrass, annoy, or upset them.

laugh at idiom ~을 비웃다, 놀리다
If people laugh at someone or something, they mock them or make jokes about them.

✵ **rack** [ræk] n. 받침대; 선반; v. 괴롭히다, 고통을 주다 (bike rack n. 자전거 고정대)
A rack is a frame or shelf, usually with bars or hooks, that is used for holding things or for hanging things on.

disgust [disgʌ́st] v. 혐오감을 유발하다, 역겹게 하다; n. 혐오감, 역겨움, 넌더리
(disgusting a. 혐오스러운, 넌더리 나는)
If you say that something is disgusting, you are criticizing it because it is extremely unpleasant.

glory [gló:ri] n. 찬란한 아름다움, 장관; 영광, 영예
The glory of something is its great beauty or impressive nature.

steal [sti:l] v. (stole—stolen) 훔치다, 도둑질하다
If you steal something from someone, you take it away from them without their permission and without intending to return it.

wonder [wʌ́ndər] v. 궁금해하다; (크게) 놀라다; n. 경탄, 경이
If you wonder about something, you think about it because it interests you and you want to know more about it.

glance [glæns] v. 흘낏 보다; 대충 훑어보다; n. 흘낏 봄
If you glance at something or someone, you look at them very quickly and then look away again immediately.

notice [nóutis] v. ~을 의식하다; 주목하다; n. 주목, 알아챔; 안내문
If you notice something or someone, you become aware of them.

bush [buʃ] n. 관목, 덤불; 우거진 것
A bush is a large plant which is smaller than a tree and has a lot of branches.

edge [edʒ] n. 끝, 가장자리; 날; v. 조금씩 움직이다
The edge of something is the place or line where it stops, or the part of it that is furthest from the middle.

yard [ja:rd] n. 마당, 뜰 (school yard n. 학교 운동장)
The school yard is the large open area with a hard surface just outside a school building, where the schoolchildren can play and do other activities.

rest [rest] v. 기대다; 쉬다; n. 나머지 (사람들 · 것들); 휴식
If you rest something somewhere, you put it there so that its weight is supported.

garbage [gá:rbidʒ] n. 쓰레기, 찌꺼기 (garbage can n. 쓰레기통)
A garbage can is a container that you put rubbish into.

give a look idiom 표정을 짓다; ~를 보다
If you give someone a look, you look at them in a particular way.

whisper [hwíspər] v. 속삭이다, 소곤거리다; n. 속삭임, 소곤거리는 소리
When you whisper, you say something very quietly.

desert [dizə́:rt] ① v. 버리다; 떠나다 ② n. 사막; a. 불모의
If you desert something that you support, use, or are involved with, you stop supporting it, using it, or being involved with it.

backpack [bǽkpæ̀k] n. 배낭
A backpack is a bag with straps that go over your shoulders, so that you can carry things on your back when you are walking or climbing.

disappear [disəpíər] v. 사라지다, 보이지 않게 되다; 실종되다, 없어지다
If you say that someone or something disappears, you mean that you can no longer see them, usually because you or they have changed position.

awful [ɔ́:fəl] a. 엄청; 끔찍한, 지독한 (awfully ad. 정말, 몹시)
You can use awful with noun groups that refer to an amount in order to emphasize how large that amount is.

poke [pouk] v. (손가락 등으로) 쿡 찌르다; 쑥 내밀다; n. 찌르기
If you poke someone or something, you quickly push them with your finger or with a sharp object.

clear one's throat idiom 헛기침을 하다
If you clear your throat, you cough once in order to make it easier to speak or to attract people's attention.

insult [insʌ́lt] v. 모욕하다; n. 모욕(적인 말·행동)
If someone insults you, they say or do something that is rude or offensive.

beat-up [bi:t-ʌ́p] a. 낡아빠진, 닳아빠진
A beat-up car or other object is old and in bad condition.

dent [dent] n. 움푹 들어간 곳, 찌그러진 곳; v. 찌그러뜨리다; (자신감·명성 등을) 훼손하다
A dent is a hollow in the surface of something which has been caused by hitting or pressing it.

scratch [skrætʃ] n. 긁힌 자국; 긁히는 소리; v. 긁다, 할퀴다; 긁히는 소리를 내다
Scratches on someone or something are small shallow cuts.

shiny [ʃáini] a. 빛나는, 반짝거리는
Shiny things are bright and reflect light.

friendly [fréndli] a. 친숙한, 상냥한; 친절한
If someone is friendly, they behave in a pleasant, kind way, and like to be with other people.

nod [nad] v. (고개를) 끄덕이다, 끄덕여 나타내다; n. (고개를) 끄덕임
If you nod, you move your head downward and upward to show agreement, understanding, or approval.

mood [muːd] n. 기분; 분위기
Your mood is the way you are feeling at a particular time.

apologize [əpálədʒàiz] v. 사과하다, 사죄하다
When you apologize to someone, you say that you are sorry that you have hurt them or caused trouble for them.

feel out of place idiom 위화감을 느끼다, 어색하게 느끼다
If someone or something feels out of place in a particular situation, they do not seem to belong there or to be suitable for that situation.

shrug [ʃrʌg] v. (어깨를) 으쓱하다; n. (어깨를) 으쓱하기
If you shrug, you raise your shoulders to show that you are not interested in something or that you do not know or care about something.

Chapter 4

1. **What was Francine thinking of while she bounced the tennis ball?**
   A. She was thinking that she could try playing tennis at school.
   B. She was thinking that she should get a dog.
   C. She was wishing for another bike.
   D. She was wishing for new friends.

2. **Why was the bike purple?**
   A. It was Francine's father's favorite color when he was her age.
   B. It was the only color they had when Francine's father was young.
   C. It was the color for the common people.
   D. It was greatly valued in modern times.

3. What happened to Francine's father in the neighborhood bike race from his childhood?

A. He won first place.

B. He broke his bike by pedaling like crazy.

C. He got in a terrible accident.

D. He came out in the middle.

4. How did her father feel about what had happened?

A. He wished he could have won first place.

B. He wished he had biked slower.

C. He wished he had gotten a faster bike.

D. He was glad that he had improved.

5. Why could Francine's father not get her a new bike?

A. They didn't have the space in their apartment.

B. They didn't have the extra money then.

C. He didn't know where to buy a new bike.

D. He wanted her to only use his old bike.

1분에 몇 단어를 읽는지 리딩 속도를 측정해보세요.

$$\frac{517 \ words}{reading \ time \ (\qquad) \ sec} \times 60 = (\qquad) \ WPM$$

Build Your Vocabulary

edge [edʒ] n. 끝, 가장자리; 날; v. 조금씩 움직이다
The edge of something is the place or line where it stops, or the part of it that is furthest from the middle.

bounce [bauns] v. 튀다, 튀기다; 흔들거리며 가다; n. 튐, 튀어 오름
When an object such as a ball bounces or when you bounce it, it moves upward from a surface or away from it immediately after hitting it.

admire [ædmáiər] v. 감탄하며 바라보다; 존경하다, 칭찬하다
If you admire someone or something, you look at them with pleasure.

pop [pap] v. 불쑥 움직이다; 펑 하고 터지다; n. 펑 (하고 터지는 소리)
If you pop somewhere, you go there for a short time.

practice [præktis] v. 연습하다; 실행하다; n. 연습, 훈련; 실행
If you practice something, you keep doing it regularly in order to be able to do it better.

coordinate [kouɔ́:rdənət] v. (몸의 움직임을) 조정하다; 조직화하다; 꾸미다; n. 좌표
(coordination n. (신체 동작의) 조정력)
Coordination is the ability to use the different parts of your body together efficiently.

coach [koutʃ] n. (스포츠 팀의) 코치; v. 코치하다, 지도하다
A coach is someone who trains a person or team of people in a particular sport.

vouch [vautʃ] v. 보증하다, 보장하다; 단언하다; 증명하다
If you vouch for something, you say that you know something is true because you have seen it yourself.

dull [dʌl] a. 따분한, 재미없는; 둔탁한; v. 둔해지다, 약해지다
(dully ad. 활발하지 못하게, 둔하게)
Someone or something that is dull is not very lively or energetic.

nod [nad] v. (고개를) 끄덕이다, 끄덕여 나타내다; n. (고개를) 끄덕임
If you nod, you move your head downward and upward to show agreement, understanding, or approval.

favorite [féivərit] a. 마음에 드는, 매우 좋아하는; n. 마음에 드는 사람; 좋아하는 물건
Your favorite thing or person of a particular type is the one you like most.

royal [rɔ́iəl] a. 국왕의; 성대한, 위풍당당한 (royalty n. 왕족)
The members of royal families are sometimes referred to as royalty.

dignify [dígnəfài] v. 위엄 있게 하다; 그럴듯하게 하다 (dignified a. 위엄 있는)
If you say that someone or something is dignified, you mean they are calm, impressive and deserve respect.

majestic [mədʒéstik] a. 위엄 있는, 장엄한; 웅장한
If you describe something or someone as majestic, you think they are very beautiful, dignified, and impressive.

value [vǽljuː] v. 소중하게 생각하다; (가치·가격을) 평가하다; n. 가치; 중요성; 값
If you value something or someone, you think that they are important and you appreciate them.

ancient [éinʃənt] a. 고대의; 아주 오래된; n. (pl.) 고대인
Ancient means belonging to the distant past, especially to the period in history before the end of the Roman Empire.

invent [invént] v. 발명하다; (사실이 아닌 것을) 지어내다
If you invent something such as a machine or process, you are the first person to think of it or make it.

^{복습}**wheel** [hwi:l] n. 바퀴; (자동차 등의) 핸들; v. (바퀴 달린 것을) 밀다; 태우고 가다
The wheels of a vehicle are the circular objects which are fixed underneath it and which enable it to move along the ground.

exact [igzǽkt] a. 정확한, 정밀한; 엄격한 (exactly ad. 맞아; 정확히, 틀림없이)
If you say 'Exactly,' you are agreeing with someone or emphasizing the truth of what they say.

^{복습}**sigh** [sai] v. 한숨을 쉬다, 한숨짓다; n. 한숨; 탄식
When you sigh, you let out a deep breath, as a way of expressing feelings such as disappointment, tiredness, or pleasure.

that figures idiom 그럴 줄 알았다, 생각한 대로이다
If you say 'That figures' or 'It figures,' you mean that the fact referred to is not surprising.

boyhood [bɔ́ihud] n. (남자의) 어린 시절
Boyhood is the period of a male person's life during which he is a boy.

be bound to idiom ～하게 마련이다; 반드시 ～하다
If you say that something is bound to happen or be true, you feel confident and certain of it.

follow [fálou] v. (결과가) 뒤따르다; (～의 뒤를) 따라가다
An event, activity, or period of time that follows a particular thing happens or comes after that thing, at a later time.

^{복습}**ride** [raid] v. (차량·자전거·말 등을) 타다; n. (차량·자전거 등을) 타고 달리기; 여정
When you ride a bicycle or a motorcycle, you sit on it, control it, and travel along on it.

handle [hǽndl] v. (차량 등이) 말을 잘 듣다; 다루다, 처리하다; n. 손잡이
If something such as a vehicle handles well, it is easy to use or control.

race [reis] n. 경주; 인종, 민족; v. 쏜살같이 가다; 경쟁하다, 경주하다
A race is a competition to see who is the fastest, for example in running, swimming, or driving.

neighborhood [néibərhùd] n. (도시의) 지역, 구역; 인근, 근처; 이웃 사람들
A neighborhood is one of the parts of a town where people live.

line up idiom 줄을 서다
If people line up, they form a line, standing one behind the other or beside each other.

brag [bræg] v. 자랑하다, 떠벌리다
If you brag, you say in a very proud way that you have something or have done something.

beat [biːt] v. (게임·시합에서) 이기다; 능가하다; 두드리다; n. 고동, 맥박; 리듬
If you beat someone in a competition or election, you defeat them.

in the worst way idiom 대단히, 몹시, 매우
If you want someone or something in the worst way, you want them very much or in an extreme degree.

pedal [pedl] v. 페달을 밟다; (자전거를) 타고 가다; n. 페달
When you pedal a bicycle, you push the pedals around with your feet to make it move.

lean [liːn] v. ~에 기대다; (몸을) 숙이다; 기울다; a. 호리호리한
If you lean on or against someone or something, you rest against them so that they partly support your weight.

improve [imprúːv] v. 개선되다, 나아지다; 향상시키다 (improvement n. 개선; 향상)
If there is an improvement in something, it becomes better.

disappoint [dìsəpɔ́int] v. 실망시키다; 좌절시키다 (disappointed a. 실망한, 낙담한)
If you are disappointed, you are rather sad because something has not happened or because something is not as good as you had hoped.

wonder [wʌ́ndər] v. 궁금해하다; (크게) 놀라다; n. 경탄, 경이
If you wonder about something, you think about it because it interests you and you want to know more about it.

definite [défənit] a. 분명한, 뚜렷한; 확실한, 확고한 (**definitely** ad. 분명히, 틀림없이)
You use definitely to emphasize that something is the case, or to emphasize the strength of your intention or opinion.

crack [kræk] v. 갈라지다, 금이 가다; 깨지다, 부서지다; n. (갈라져 생긴) 금; 날카로운 소리
If something hard cracks, or if you crack it, it becomes slightly damaged, with lines appearing on its surface.

grin [grin] v. 활짝 웃다; n. 활짝 웃음
When you grin, you smile broadly.

extra [ékstrə] a. 추가의; n. 추가되는 것; ad. 추가로
You use extra to describe an amount, person, or thing that is added to others of the same kind, or that can be added to others of the same kind.

proud [praud] a. 자랑스러워하는; 자존심이 강한; 오만한, 거만한
If you feel proud, you feel pleased about something good that you possess or have done, or about something good that a person close to you has done.

history [hístəri] n. 역사; 역사(학)
You can refer to the events of the past as history. You can also refer to the past events which concern a particular topic or place as its history.

afraid [əfréid] a. 걱정하는; 두려워하는, 겁내는
If you want to apologize to someone or to disagree with them in a polite way, you can say 'I'm afraid.'

satisfy [sǽtisfài] v. 만족시키다; 채우다
If someone or something satisfies you, they give you enough of what you want or need to make you pleased or contented.

be a long way from idiom ~와 거리가 멀다; 멀리 떨어져 있다
If you say that something is a long way from being true, you are emphasizing that it is definitely not true.

Chapter 5

1. **How did Francine feel the next morning?**

   A. She was excited for a brand new day.

   B. She felt just as bad as she had the day before.

   C. She felt that she was going to change things.

   D. She felt sick and decided to stay home from school.

2. **What did the garbage collectors do to Francine's bike?**

   A. They left it in the bushes.

   B. They moved it to the bike rack.

   C. They threw it into the truck.

   D. They rode around on it.

3. **What did Francine tell Arthur and Buster had happened to her bike?**

   A. She told them that it had been stolen.

   B. She told them that she had thrown it away.

   C. She told them that the garbage collectors had taken it.

   D. She told them that it had been replaced with a new one.

4. **Why did Muffy think that Francine's bike might have been stolen?**

   A. She thought that it might have looked like trash.

   B. She thought that it was so old that it might have been an antique.

   C. She thought that someone might have thought that nobody wanted it.

   D. She thought that it was important to a gang of international bike thieves.

5. **Who did Francine not want to get involved in her problem?**

   A. The principal

   B. Her parents

   C. Arthur

   D. Muffy

$$\frac{525 \ words}{reading \ time \ (\qquad) \ sec} \times 60 = (\qquad) \ WPM$$

Build Your Vocabulary

up ahead [ʌp əhéd] ad. 그 앞쪽에
If someone or something is up ahead, they are not far in front.

bush [buʃ] n. 관목, 덤불; 우거진 것
A bush is a large plant which is smaller than a tree and has a lot of branches.

block [blak] v. 막다, 차단하다; 방해하다; n. 사각형 덩어리; 구역, 블록
If something blocks your view, it prevents you from seeing something because it is between you and that thing.

garbage [gáːrbidʒ] n. 쓰레기, 찌꺼기 (garbage truck n. 쓰레기 수거차)
A garbage truck is a large truck which collects the garbage from outside people's houses.

collector [kəléktər] n. 수집가; 징수원 (garbage collector n. 쓰레기 수거인)
A garbage collector is a person whose job is to take people's garbage away.

trash [træʃ] n. 쓰레기; v. 부수다, 엉망으로 만들다; 맹비난하다 (trash can n. 쓰레기통)
A trash can is a large round container which people put their rubbish in and which is usually kept outside their house.

wave [weiv] v. 흔들다; 손짓하다; n. 파도, 물결; (팔·손·몸을) 흔들기
If you wave or wave your hand, you move your hand from side to side in the air, usually in order to say hello or goodbye to someone.

‡ **roar** [rɔːr] n. 굉음; 으르렁거림; 함성; v. 으르렁거리다; 고함치다
A roar is a loud noise made by something such as an engine or a storm.

pull away idiom 움직이기 시작하다, 떠나다
When a vehicle pulls away, it begins to move.

복습 **attention** [əténʃən] n. 주의, 주목; 관심 (get one's attention idiom ~의 관심을 얻다)
If someone or something gets your attention, they make you notice them.

come to a stop idiom 서다, 멈추다
If something that is moving comes to a stop, it slows down and no longer moves.

‡ **breathe** [briːð] v. 호흡하다, 숨을 쉬다
When people or animals breathe, they take air into their lungs and let it out again.

‡ **terrible** [térəbl] a. 끔찍한, 소름 끼치는; 지독한; 엄청난
A terrible experience or situation is very serious or very unpleasant.

‡‡ **imagine** [imædʒin] v. 상상하다, (마음속으로) 그리다
If you imagine something, you think about it and your mind forms a picture or idea of it.

복습 **yard** [jaːrd] n. 마당, 뜰 (school yard n. 학교 운동장)
The school yard is the large open area with a hard surface just outside a school building, where the schoolchildren can play and do other activities.

zoom [zuːm] v. 쌩 하고 가다; 급등하다, 급증하다; n. 쌩 하고 지나가는 소리
If you zoom somewhere, you go there very quickly.

복습 **brake** [breik] v. 브레이크를 밟다; 속도를 줄이다; n. 브레이크, 제동 장치; 제동
When a vehicle or its driver brakes, or when a driver brakes a vehicle, the driver makes it slow down or stop by using the brakes.

be rid of idiom 벗어나다, 해방되다
If you are rid of someone or something that you did not want or that caused problems for you, they are no longer with you or causing problems for you.

comfortable [kʌ́mfərtəbl] a. 편하게 생각하는; 편안한, 쾌적한; 넉넉한
If you feel comfortable with a particular situation or person, you feel confident and relaxed with them.

lose track of idiom ~을 놓치다, 잊다
If you lose track of someone or something, you no longer know where they are or what is happening.

stuff [stʌf] n. 것(들), 물건; v. 채워 넣다; 쑤셔 넣다
You can use stuff to refer to things such as a substance, a collection of things, events, or ideas, or the contents of something in a general way without mentioning the thing itself by name.

steal [stiːl] v. (stole-stolen) 훔치다, 도둑질하다
If you steal something from someone, you take it away from them without their permission and without intending to return it.

pause [pɔːz] v. (말·일을 하다가) 잠시 멈추다; 정지시키다; n. 멈춤
If you pause while you are doing something, you stop for a short period and then continue.

confuse [kənfjúːz] v. (사람을) 혼란시키다; 혼동하다 (confused a. 혼란스러워 하는)
If you are confused, you do not know exactly what is happening or what to do.

shrug [ʃrʌg] v. (어깨를) 으쓱하다; n. (어깨를) 으쓱하기
If you shrug, you raise your shoulders to show that you are not interested in something or that you do not know or care about something.

gasp [gæsp] v. 숨이 턱 막히다, 헉 하고 숨을 쉬다; n. 헉 하는 소리를 냄
When you gasp, you take a short quick breath through your mouth, especially when you are surprised, shocked, or in pain.

antique [æntíːk] n. 골동품; a. (귀중한) 골동품인
An antique is an old object such as a piece of china or furniture which is valuable because of its beauty or rarity.

bet [bet] v. 틀림없다, 분명하다; (내기 등에) 돈을 걸다; n. 내기; 짐작
You use expressions such as 'I bet,' 'I'll bet,' and 'you can bet' to indicate that you are sure something is true.

gang [gæŋ] n. 갱, 범죄 조직; 패거리
A gang is a group of criminals who work together to commit crimes.

international [intərnǽʃənəl] a. 국제적인
International means between or involving different countries.

thief [θiːf] n. (pl. thieves) 도둑, 절도범
A thief is a person who steals something from another person.

black market [blæk máːrkit] n. 암시장; v. ~을 암시장에서 팔다
If something is bought or sold on the black market, it is bought or sold illegally.

calm down idiom 진정하다, 흥분을 가라앉히다
If someone calms down, or you calm them down, they stop being angry or excited and become calm.

panic [pǽnik] v. 겁에 질려 어쩔 줄 모르다, 공황 상태에 빠지다; n. 극심한 공포, 공황
If you panic or if someone panics you, you suddenly feel anxious or afraid, and act quickly and without thinking carefully.

drag [dræg] v. (원치 않는 곳에) 가게 하다; 끌다; 힘들게 움직이다; n. 끌기; 장애물
(drag into idiom ~을 끌어들이다)
If you drag someone into something, you make them become involved in a difficult or unpleasant situation when they do not want to be involved.

principal [prínsəpəl] n. 교장; 학장, 총장; a. 주요한, 주된
The principal of a school is the person in charge of the school.

Chapter 6

1. **What did Francine say she did that impressed the Brain?**

    A. She hurried home to do her chores.

    B. She finished her homework early.

    C. She stopped by the library after school.

    D. She threw a fastball in last night's baseball game.

2. **How did Francine say that her bike was stolen?**

    A. Some men grabbed it while it was parked at the Sugar Bowl.

    B. Someone had stolen it from the bike rack during school.

    C. A truck with a claw grabbed it while she was riding it.

    D. A garbage collector threw it into his truck.

3. What did Buster suggest should be done about Francine's bike?

A. Her friends should let her borrow their bikes for a while.

B. They should tell her parents what had happened.

C. They should have the state police blanket the highways.

D. They should have a private investigator take on the case.

4. Why did Francine go home early from school?

A. She had forgotten her lunch at home.

B. She had forgotten her homework at home.

C. She didn't want to be around her mean friends anymore.

D. She wasn't feeling well and the nurse let her go home.

5. Why did Francine's friends think that she might have made up the story about the truck?

A. She had been watching too many crime TV shows lately.

B. She wanted to keep them from finding out who really took her bike.

C. She had been reading too many science fiction books lately.

D. She was too embarrassed to admit that she had thrown it away.

1분에 몇 단어를 읽는지 리딩 속도를 측정해보세요.

$$\frac{532 \ words}{reading \ time \ (\quad) \ sec} \times 60 = (\quad) \ WPM$$

Build Your Vocabulary

get straight idiom 분명히 하다; ~을 명쾌하게 이해하다
If you get something straight, you make sure that you understand it properly or that someone else does.

∗ chore [ʧɔːr] n. (pl.) (가정의) 잡일, 허드렛일; 따분한 일
Chores are tasks such as cleaning, washing, and ironing that have to be done regularly at home.

nod [nad] v. (고개를) 끄덕이다, 끄덕여 나타내다; n. (고개를) 끄덕임
If you nod, you move your head downward and upward to show agreement, understanding, or approval.

∗ impress [imprés] v. 깊은 인상을 주다, 감명을 주다; 새기다 (impressed a. 감명을 받은)
If something impresses you, you feel great admiration for it.

whisper [hwíspər] v. 속삭이다, 소곤거리다; n. 속삭임, 소곤거리는 소리
When you whisper, you say something very quietly.

scratch [skræʧ] v. 긁다, 할퀴다; 긁히는 소리를 내다; n. 긁힌 자국; 긁히는 소리
If you scratch yourself, you rub your fingernails against your skin because it is itching.

chin [ʧin] n. 턱
Your chin is the part of your face that is below your mouth and above your neck.

ride [raid] v. (차량·자전거·말 등을) 타다; n. (차량·자전거 등을) 타고 달리기; 여정
When you ride a bicycle or a motorcycle, you sit on it, control it, and travel along on it.

whistle [hwisl] v. 휘파람을 불다; 호루라기를 불다; n. 호루라기; 호루라기 소리; 휘파람
When you whistle or when you whistle a tune, you make a series of musical notes by forcing your breath out between your lips, or your teeth.

all of a sudden idiom 갑자기
If something happens all of a sudden, it happens quickly and unexpectedly.

claw [klɔ:] n. 갈고리 모양의 도구; (동물의) 발톱; v. (손톱·발톱으로) 할퀴다
A claw is a mechanical device that is curved or bent to suspend or hold or pull something.

reach [ri:ʃ] v. (손·팔을) 뻗다, 내밀다; 이르다, 도달하다; n. 거리; 범위
If you reach somewhere, you move your arm and hand to take or touch something.

grab [græb] v. 붙잡다, 움켜잡다; n. 와락 잡아채려고 함
If you grab something, you take it or pick it up suddenly and roughly.

lift [lift] v. 들어올리다, 올리다; n. (들어)올리기; (차 등을) 태워 주기
If you lift something, you move it to another position, especially upward.

drop [drap] v. 떨어뜨리다; 약해지다, 낮추다; (사람·짐을) 내리다; n. 방울; 하락, 감소
If you drop something somewhere or if it drops there, you deliberately let it fall there.

speed [spi:d] v. (sped/speeded–sped/speeded) 빨리 가다; 속도 위반을 하다; n. (물체의 이동) 속도
If you speed somewhere, you move or travel there quickly, usually in a vehicle.

fist [fist] n. (쥔) 주먹
Your hand is referred to as your fist when you have bent your fingers in toward the palm in order to hit someone.

suppose [səpóuz] v. (~이라고) 생각하다, 추측하다; 가정하다
If you suppose that something is true, you believe that it is probably true, because of other things that you know.

license [láisəns] n. 면허(증); 자격; v. (공적으로) 허가하다
A license is an official document which gives you permission to do, use, or own something.

plate [pleit] n. (자동차) 번호판; 접시, 그릇; 판, 패; v. 판을 대다
(license plate n. (자동차) 번호판)
A license plate is a sign on the front and back of a vehicle that shows its license number.

concern [kənsə́:rn] v. ~를 걱정스럽게 하다; 영향을 미치다; n. 우려; 배려
(concerned a. 걱정하는, 염려하는)
If something concerns you, it worries you.

roam [roum] v. (이리저리) 돌아다니다, 배회하다; 천천히 훑다
If you roam an area or roam around it, you wander or travel around it without having a particular purpose.

put out idiom 발표하다; 내놓다
To put out something means to produce information and make it available for everyone to read or hear.

bulletin [búlitən] n. (중요한) 고시, 공고; 뉴스 단신
A bulletin is a short official announcement made publicly to inform people about an important matter.

state [steit] n. 주(州); 국가, 나라; 상태; v. 말하다, 진술하다; 명시하다
(state police n. 주립 경찰)
Some large countries such as the USA are divided into smaller areas called states.

blanket [blǽŋkit] v. (완전히) 뒤덮다; n. 담요; a. 전반적, 전면적
If something such as snow blankets an area, it covers it.

highway [háiwèi] n. 고속도로
A highway is a main road, especially one that connects towns or cities.

^{복습}**rest** [rest] n. 휴식; 나머지 (사람들·것들); v. 쉬다; 기대다
(rest stop n. (간선 도로변의) 주차장, 휴게소)
A rest stop is a place beside a motorway or freeway where you can buy gas and other things, or have a meal.

^{복습}**comfortable** [kʌ́mfərtəbl] a. 편하게 생각하는; 편안한, 쾌적한; 넉넉한
(uncomfortable a. 불편한, 거북한)
If you are uncomfortable, you are slightly worried or embarrassed, and not relaxed and confident.

^복**pale** [peil] a. 창백한, 핼쑥한; (색깔이) 엷은; v. 창백해지다, 핼쑥해지다
If someone looks pale, their face looks a lighter color than usual, usually because they are ill, frightened, or shocked.

check out idiom ~을 확인하다; (흥미로운 것을) 살펴보다
If you check someone or something out, you examine them in order to be certain that everything is correct, true, or satisfactory.

fishy [fíʃi] a. 수상한 (냄새가 나는); 생선 냄새가 나는
If you describe a situation as fishy, you feel that someone is not telling the truth or behaving completely honestly.

^{복습}**survive** [sərváiv] v. 견뎌 내다; 살아남다, 생존하다
If you survive in difficult circumstances, you manage to live or continue in spite of them and do not let them affect you very much.

^{복습}**terrible** [térəbl] a. 끔찍한, 소름 끼치는; 지독한; 엄청난
A terrible experience or situation is very serious or very unpleasant.

ordeal [ɔːrdíːəl] n. (힘들거나 불쾌한) 시련, 경험
If you describe an experience or situation as an ordeal, you think it is difficult and unpleasant.

take it from me idiom 정말이다, 내 말은 믿어도 된다
You can say 'take it from me' to tell someone that you are absolutely sure that what you are saying is correct, and that they should believe you.

add up idiom 말이 되다, 앞뒤가 맞다

If a situation does not add up, there is no reasonable or likely explanation for it.

expect [ikspékt] v. 예상하다, 기대하다; 요구하다

If you expect something to happen, you believe that it will happen.

dumb [dʌm] a. 멍청한, 바보 같은; 말을 못 하는

If you call a person dumb, you mean that they are stupid or foolish.

refer [rifə́:r] v. 언급하다; 지시하다, 나타내다; 참조하게 하다

If you refer to a particular subject or person, you talk about them or mention them.

unlikely [ʌnláikli] a. ~할 것 같지 않은, 있음직하지 않은; 예상 밖의

If you say that something is unlikely to happen or unlikely to be true, you believe that it will not happen or that it is not true, although you are not completely sure.

invent [invént] v. (사실이 아닌 것을) 지어내다; 발명하다

If you invent a story or excuse, you try to make other people believe that it is true when in fact it is not.

punish [pʌ́niʃ] v. 처벌하다, 벌주다

To punish someone means to make them suffer in some way because they have done something wrong.

thief [θiːf] n. 도둑, 절도범

A thief is a person who steals something from another person.

Chapter 7

1. **How did Francine's father react to Francine's story about the truck with a giant claw?**

   A. He wasn't paying much attention.

   B. He told her it sounded unbelievable.

   C. He was glad that Francine was okay.

   D. He was horrified that such a truck existed.

2. **What was Francine's sister, Catherine, doing while her family watched TV?**

   A. She was working on homework.

   B. She was reading a book.

   C. She was doing her hair.

   D. She was painting her nails.

3. **Why did Francine's father tell Francine to not give up hope?**

   A. He said that the bike might find its way back to them.

   B. He said that he would buy her a new bike after all.

   C. He said that they would go searching for the bike.

   D. He said that he would get her a new dog instead.

4. **Why did Francine tell Catherine that she didn't go right to the police?**

   A. She said that she went to her friends first.

   B. She said that the police were too far away.

   C. She said that she was afraid of the police.

   D. She said that she fell off her bike and got amnesia.

5. **How did Catherine react to Francine's explanation for not going to the police?**

   A. She said that she would have gone to the police.

   B. She said that Francine's story was from the movie they saw last week.

   C. She said that nobody would believe her explanation.

   D. She said that she would have done the same thing.

1분에 몇 단어를 읽는지 리딩 속도를 측정해보세요.

$$\frac{518 \text{ words}}{\text{reading time (} \qquad \text{) sec}} \times 60 = (\qquad) \text{ WPM}$$

Build Your Vocabulary

get through idiom ～에게 전달되다; ～을 하다, 끝내다; 써 버리다
If you get through to someone, you succeed in communicating with someone in a meaningful way.

go on idiom 말을 계속하다; (어떤 상황이) 계속되다; 시작하다
When you go on, you continue speaking after a short pause.

breath [breθ] n. 숨, 입김 (take a deep breath idiom 심호흡하다)
When you take a deep breath, you breathe in a lot of air at one time.

steal [sti:l] v. (stole-stolen) 훔치다, 도둑질하다
If you steal something from someone, you take it away from them without their permission and without intending to return it.

claw [klɔ:] n. 갈고리 모양의 도구; (동물의) 발톱; v. (손톱·발톱으로) 할퀴다
A claw is a mechanical device that is curved or bent to suspend or hold or pull something.

knock [nak] v. 치다, 부딪치다; (문을) 두드리다; n. 문 두드리는 소리; 부딪침
(knock off idiom ～을 쳐서 떨어뜨리다)
To knock off someone means to make them fall off something by hitting them.

goodness [gúdnis] int. (놀람을 나타내어) 와, 어머나!
People sometimes say 'goodness' or 'my goodness' to express surprise.

attention [əténʃən] n. 주의, 주목; 관심 (**pay attention** idiom 주의를 기울이다)
If you pay attention to someone, you watch them, listen to them, or take notice of them.

close call [klóus kɔ:l] n. 위기일발, 아슬아슬한 상황
If you describe an event as a close call, you mean that an accident or a disaster very nearly happened.

unbelievable [ʌnbilí:vəbl] a. 믿기 어려울 정도인; 믿기 힘든
You can use unbelievable to emphasize that you think something is very bad or shocking.

fingernail [fíŋgərneil] n. 손톱
Your fingernails are the thin hard areas at the end of each of your fingers.

squirm [skwə:rm] v. 꼼지락대다; 몹시 창피해 하다
If you squirm, you move your body from side to side, usually because you are nervous or uncomfortable.

tough [tʌf] a. 힘든, 어려운; 억센, 거친; 엄한, 냉정한
A tough way of life or period of time is difficult or full of suffering.

throw up idiom 토하다, 게우다
When someone throws up, they bring food they have eaten back out of their mouth.

concentrate [kánsəntrèit] v. (정신을) 집중하다; 농축하다; n. 농축물
If you concentrate on something, you give all your attention to it.

nail [neil] n. 손톱; 못; v. 못으로 박다
Your nails are the thin hard parts that grow at the ends of your fingers and toes.

spot [spat] n. (작은) 점; 곳, 장소; 얼룩; v. 발견하다, 찾다, 알아채다
Spots are small, round, colored areas on a surface.

frantic [frǽntik] a. 제정신이 아닌; 정신 없이 서두는
(frantically ad. 미친 듯이, 극도로 흥분하여)
If you are frantic, you are behaving in a wild and uncontrolled way because you are frightened or worried.

inspect [inspékt] v. 점검하다, 검사하다; 사찰하다
If you inspect something, you look at every part of it carefully in order to find out about it or check that it is all right.

let out idiom (울음소리·신음소리 등을) 내다, 지르다
To let out something means to suddenly make a loud sound such as a shout or cry.

sigh [sai] n. 한숨; 탄식; v. 한숨을 쉬다, 한숨짓다
A sigh is a long, deep audible exhalation expressing sadness, relief, or tiredness.

blink [bliŋk] v. 눈을 깜박이다; (불빛이) 깜박거리다; n. 눈을 깜박거림
When you blink or when you blink your eyes, you shut your eyes and very quickly open them again.

be about to idiom 막 ~하려던 참이다
If you are about to do something, you are going to do it very soon.

give up idiom 단념하다; 그만두다; 포기하다
If you give up something, you stop trying to do it or having it.

roll one's eyes idiom 눈을 굴리다
If you roll your eyes, you move them round and upward when you are frightened, bored, or annoyed.

extra [ékstrə] a. 추가의; n. 추가되는 것; ad. 추가로
You use extra to describe an amount, person, or thing that is added to others of the same kind, or that can be added to others of the same kind.

rest [rest] n. 휴식; 나머지 (사람들·것들); v. 쉬다; 기대다
If you get some rest or have a rest, you do not do anything active for a time.

stick out idiom ~을 내밀다, 튀어나오게 하다
If you stick something out, you make something, especially part of your body, come through a hole.

tongue [tʌŋ] n. 혀
Your tongue is the soft movable part inside your mouth which you use for tasting, eating, and speaking.

brush [brʌʃ] v. 솔질을 하다; (솔이나 손으로) 털다; n. 붓; 솔; 비
If you brush something or brush something such as dirt off it, you clean it or tidy it using a brush.

amnesia [æmníːʒə] n. 기억 상실(증)
If someone is suffering from amnesia, they have lost their memory.

firm [fəːrm] a. 단호한, 단단한; 확고한; v. 단단하게 하다; 안정되다 (firmly ad. 세게, 단단히)
If something is firm, it does not shake or move when you put weight or pressure on it, because it is strongly made or securely fastened.

stare [stɛər] v. 빤히 쳐다보다, 응시하다; n. 빤히 쳐다보기, 응시
If you stare at someone or something, you look at them for a long time.

ceiling [síːliŋ] n. 천장
A ceiling is the horizontal surface that forms the top part or roof inside a room.

imagine [imǽdʒin] v. 상상하다, (마음속으로) 그리다
If you imagine something, you think about it and your mind forms a picture or idea of it.

crash [kræʃ] v. 부딪치다; 충돌하다; 굉음을 내다; n. 요란한 소리; (자동차·항공기) 사고
If something crashes somewhere, it moves and hits something else violently, making a loud noise.

grab [græb] v. 붙잡다, 움켜잡다; n. 와락 잡아채려고 함
If you grab something, you take it or pick it up suddenly and roughly.

Chapter 8

1. **What news did Buster and Muffy have for Francine on their way to school?**

   A. They had found her bike.

   B. They had got her a new bike.

   C. They knew what had happened to her bike.

   D. They had found the truck that took her bike.

2. **Who did Francine's friends think had stolen her bike?**

   A. A garbage collector

   B. Francine's father

   C. Buster

   D. Binky

3. **Why did they think that person stole her bike?**
   A. He really liked that bike.

   B. He was big enough to steal a whole bike.

   C. He knew it was worth a lot of money.

   D. He thought it might have been trash.

4. **What did Muffy want a volunteer from the crowd of students to do?**
   A. She wanted a volunteer to threaten Binky to confess.

   B. She wanted a volunteer to help find Francine's bike.

   C. She wanted a volunteer to buy a new bike for Francine.

   D. She wanted a volunteer to talk to Francine's father about the bike.

5. **Why did Francine's friends feel bad?**
   A. They had embarrassed Francine.

   B. They had wrongly accused Binky.

   C. They had gotten Francine in trouble.

   D. They had no idea how to get Francine's bike back.

1분에 몇 단어를 읽는지 리딩 속도를 측정해보세요.

$$\frac{569 \text{ words}}{\text{reading time (} \qquad \text{) sec}} \times 60 = (\qquad) \text{ WPM}$$

Build Your Vocabulary

☆ **crime** [kraim] n. 범행, 범죄
A crime is an illegal action or activity for which a person can be punished by law.

복습 **century** [séntʃəri] n. 1세기, 100년
A century is any period of a hundred years.

복습 **frown** [fraun] v. 얼굴을 찌푸리다; n. 찡그림, 찌푸림
When someone frowns, their eyebrows become drawn together, because they are annoyed or puzzled.

⋆ **fool** [fu:l] v. 속이다, 기만하다; 바보 짓을 하다; n. 바보
If someone fools you, they deceive or trick you.

복습 **nod** [nad] v. (고개를) 끄덕이다, 끄덕여 나타내다; n. (고개를) 끄덕임
If you nod, you move your head downward and upward to show agreement, understanding, or approval.

make up idiom (이야기 등을) 만들어 내다; ~을 이루다, 형성하다
If you make up something, you invent something artificial or untrue, often in order to trick someone.

⋆ **dizzy** [dízi] a. 현기증 나는; 아찔한
If you feel dizzy, you feel that you are losing your balance and are about to fall.

protect [prətékt] v. 보호하다, 지키다
To protect someone or something means to prevent them from being harmed or damaged.

draw [drɔː] v. 그리다; (부드럽게) 끌어당기다; (사람의 마음을) 끌다; n. 추첨, 제비 뽑기
(drawing n. 그림, 소묘)
A drawing is a picture made with a pencil or pen.

swipe [swaip] v. 훔치다, 슬쩍 하다; 후려치다; n. 휘두르기; 비판, 비난
If you swipe something, you steal it quickly.

steal [stiːl] v. 훔치다, 도둑질하다
If you steal something from someone, you take it away from them without their permission and without intending to return it.

never mind idiom (중요하지 않으니까) 신경 쓰지 마, 괜찮아
You use 'never mind' to tell someone not to do something or worry about something, because it is not important.

injustice [indʒʌ́stis] n. 부당함, 부당성; 불평등
Injustice is a lack of fairness in a situation.

bunch [bʌnʧ] n. (한 무리의) 사람들; 다발, 송이; v. 단단해지다; 단단히 접히다
A bunch of people is a group of people who share one or more characteristics or who are doing something together.

wave [weiv] v. 흔들다; 손짓하다; n. 파도, 물결; (팔·손·몸을) 흔들기
If you wave something, you hold it up and move it rapidly from side to side.

poster [póustər] n. (안내·홍보용) 포스터; (벽에 붙이는) 대형 그림
A poster is a large notice or picture that you stick on a wall or board, often in order to advertise something.

crowd [kraud] n. 사람들, 군중, 무리; v. 가득 메우다; (생각이 마음속에) 밀려오다
A crowd is a large group of people who have gathered together, for example to watch or listen to something interesting, or to protest about something.

confess [kənfés] v. (죄·잘못을) 자백하다; 고백하다, 인정하다

If someone confesses to doing something wrong, they admit that they did it.

threaten [θretn] v. 협박하다; (나쁜 일이 있을) 조짐을 보이다; 위태롭게 하다

If a person threatens to do something unpleasant to you, or if they threaten you, they say or imply that they will do something unpleasant to you, especially if you do not do what they want.

volunteer [vàləntíər] n. 자원해서 하는 사람; 자원 봉사자; v. 자원하다

A volunteer is someone who offers to do a particular task or job without being forced to do it.

go on idiom 말을 계속하다; (어떤 상황이) 계속되다; 시작하다

When you go on, you continue speaking after a short pause.

notice [nóutis] v. ~을 의식하다; 주목하다; n. 주목; 안내문

If you notice something or someone, you become aware of them.

interrupt [ìntərʌ́pt] v. (말·행동을) 방해하다, 가로막다; 중단시키다; 차단하다

If you interrupt someone who is speaking, you say or do something that causes them to stop.

traumatize [tráumətàiz] v. 정신적 외상을 초래하다, 엄청난 충격을 주다

If someone is traumatized by an event or situation, it shocks or upsets them very much, and may cause them psychological damage.

sniff [snif] v. 코를 훌쩍이다; 콧방귀를 뀌다; n. 냄새 맡기; 콧방귀 뀌기

When you sniff, you breathe in air through your nose hard enough to make a sound, for example when you are trying not to cry, or in order to show disapproval.

deed [diːd] n. 행위, 행동; 증서

A deed is something that is done, especially something that is very good or very bad.

punish [pʌ́niʃ] v. 처벌하다, 벌주다 (unpunished a. 처벌받지 않는)

If a criminal or crime goes unpunished, the criminal is not punished.

§ terrible [térəbl] a. 엄청난; 끔찍한, 소름 끼치는; 지독한
You use terrible to emphasize the great extent or degree of something.

so be it idiom 그렇다면 알겠다, 그렇게 해
The expression, 'so be it' is used to show that you accept a situation but do not like it.

＊glare [glɛər] v. 노려보다; 눈부시다; n. 노려봄; 눈부심
If you glare at someone, you look at them with an angry expression on your face.

＊guilty [gílti] a. 죄책감이 드는, 가책을 느끼는; 유죄의
If you feel guilty, you feel unhappy because you think that you have done something wrong or have failed to do something which you should have done.

＊demand [dimǽnd] v. 강력히 묻다, 따지다; 필요로 하다; n. 요구; 수요
If you demand something such as information or action, you ask for it in a very forceful way.

§ shrug [ʃrʌg] v. (어깨를) 으쓱하다; n. (어깨를) 으쓱하기
If you shrug, you raise your shoulders to show that you are not interested in something or that you do not know or care about something.

§ pick on idiom ~을 괴롭히다; 비난하다; ~을 선택하다
If you pick on someone, you treat someone badly or unfairly, especially repeatedly.

＊grunt [grʌnt] v. 으르렁거리듯 말하다; (돼지가) 꿀꿀거리다; n. 투덜대는 소리
If you grunt, you make a low sound, especially because you are annoyed or not interested in something.

§ trash [træʃ] n. 쓰레기; v. 부수다, 엉망으로 만들다; 맹비난하다
Trash consists of unwanted things or waste material such as used paper, empty containers and bottles, and waste food.

＊accident [ǽksidənt] n. 우연; 사고, 재해 (by accident idiom 우연히)
If something happens by accident, it happens completely by chance.

drop [drap] v. 떨어뜨리다; 약해지다, 낮추다; (사람·짐을) 내리다; n. 방울; 하락, 감소

If you drop something, you accidentally let it fall.

tough [tʌf] a. 억센, 거친; 힘든, 어려운; 엄한, 냉정한

A tough person is strong and determined, and can tolerate difficulty or suffering.

all of a sudden idiom 갑자기

If something happens all of a sudden, it happens quickly and unexpectedly.

join the club idiom 같은 신세가 되다; 나도 마찬가지야, 나 역시 그래

You can say 'join the club' for telling someone that you understand an unpleasant situation they are in, because you are in the same situation.

Chapter 9

1. **What story was Francine going to try to tell her father that caused Catherine to laugh?**

   A. The thieves had dropped her bike at the dump to throw the police off their trail.

   B. The thieves had dropped her bike back at school to make up for stealing it.

   C. The thieves had dropped her bike at the dump since it was as good as trash.

   D. The thieves had dropped her bike at the dump to hide it for later.

2. **Why did Francine's father not say anything even though he knew about her bike?**

   A. He had doubted himself and his ideas.

   B. He wanted her to say something first.

C. He wanted to have more time to save money for a new bike.

D. He wanted Francine to solve her own problems.

3. Why did Francine say that she lied to her father about the bike?

A. She didn't want to hurt his feelings.

B. She didn't want him to be angry with her.

C. She didn't want to be punished for losing the bike.

D. She didn't want to have to use the old bike anymore.

4. What was part of Francine's punishment?

A. She had to wash her bike.

B. She had to be nice to her sister.

C. She had to find her bike in the trash.

D. She had to come home right after school.

5. According to Francine, what was one good thing about an old bike?

A. It could sit in the dump and not look any worse.

B. It could be thrown away and not smell any worse.

C. It would be found easily in the dump.

D. It could not be broken in a garbage truck.

1분에 몇 단어를 읽는지 리딩 속도를 측정해보세요.

$$\frac{542 \ words}{reading \ time \ (\quad) \ sec} \times 60 = (\quad) \ WPM$$

Build Your Vocabulary

set [set] v. (해·달이) 지다; (시계·기기를) 맞추다; a. 위치한; 정해진
When the sun sets, it goes below the horizon.

start off idiom 움직이기 시작하다
If someone or something starts off for somewhere, they begin to move or travel to get there.

dump [dʌmp] n. (쓰레기) 폐기장; v. 버리다; ~을 떠넘기다
A dump is a place where rubbish is left, for example on open ground outside a town.

thief [θiːf] n. (pl. thieves) 도둑, 절도범
A thief is a person who steals something from another person.

drop [drɑp] v. (사람·짐을) 내리다; 떨어뜨리다; 약해지다, 낮추다; n. 방울; 하락, 감소
If you drop someone or something somewhere, you take them somewhere and leave them there, usually in a car or other vehicle.

throw off the trail idiom (뒤따르는) ~을 따돌리다
To throw someone off the trail means to stop them from finding you by using a clever plan or trick.

ridiculous [ridíkjuləs] a. 말도 안 되는, 터무니없는, 웃기는
If you say that something or someone is ridiculous, you mean that they are very foolish.

accident [ǽksidənt] n. 우연; 사고, 재해
If someone has an accident, something unpleasant happens to them that was not intended, sometimes causing injury or death.

technical [téknikəl] a. 구체적인; 전문적인; 과학 기술의, 기술적인
Technical means based on a strict way of understanding or explaining a law or rule.

fault [fɔːlt] n. 잘못, 책임; 단점; 결함; v. 나무라다, 흠잡다
If a bad or undesirable situation is your fault, you caused it or are responsible for it.

admit [ædmít] v. 인정하다, 시인하다
If you admit that something bad, unpleasant, or embarrassing is true, you agree, often unwillingly, that it is true.

proud [praud] a. 자랑스러워하는; 자존심이 강한; 오만한, 거만한
If you feel proud, you feel pleased about something good that you possess or have done, or about something good that a person close to you has done.

make fun of idiom ~을 놀리다, ~을 비웃다
If you make fun of someone or something, you laugh at them, tease them, or make jokes about them in a way that causes them to seem ridiculous.

throw away idiom (더 이상 필요 없는 것을) 버리다, 없애다
To throw away means to get rid of something that has no use or that you no longer need.

garbage [gáːrbidʒ] n. 쓰레기, 찌꺼기 (garbage truck n. 쓰레기 수거차)
A garbage truck is a large truck which collects the garbage from outside people's houses.

solve [salv] v. (문제·곤경을) 해결하다; (수학 문제 등을) 풀다
If you solve a problem or a question, you find a solution or an answer to it.

excuse [ikskjúːz] n. 변명, 이유; 핑계 거리; v. 용서하다; 변명하다; 양해를 구하다

An excuse is a reason which you give in order to explain why something has been done or has not been done, or in order to avoid doing something.

guard [gaːrd] n. 경비 요원, 보초; v. 지키다, 보호하다, 경비를 보다

A guard is a specially organized group of people, such as soldiers or policemen, who protect or watch someone or something.

point [pɔint] v. (길을) 알려 주다; (손가락 등으로) 가리키다; n. 의미; 요점

If something points to a place or points in a particular direction, it shows where that place is or it faces in that direction.

trash [træʃ] n. 쓰레기; v. 부수다, 엉망으로 만들다; 맹비난하다

Trash consists of unwanted things or waste material such as used paper, empty containers and bottles, and waste food.

hunt [hʌnt] v. (찾기 힘든 것을) 찾다; 사냥하다; n. (사람·사물을 찾는) 수색; 사냥

If you hunt for something or someone, you try to find them by searching carefully or thoroughly.

nod [nad] v. (고개를) 끄덕이다, 끄덕여 나타내다; n. (고개를) 끄덕임

If you nod, you move your head downward and upward to show agreement, understanding, or approval.

consider [kənsídər] v. 여기다; 고려하다, 숙고하다

If you consider a person or thing to be something, you have the opinion that this is what they are.

punish [pʌ́niʃ] v. 처벌하다, 벌주다 (**punishment** n. 벌, 처벌, 형벌)

To punish someone means to make them suffer in some way because they have done something wrong.

stand out idiom 눈에 띄다; ~로서 두드러지다; 뛰어나다

To stand out means to be highly noticeable.

poke [pouk] v. (손가락 등으로) 쿡 찌르다; 쑥 내밀다; n. 찌르기

If you poke someone or something, you quickly push them with your finger or with a sharp object.

stick [stik] n. 막대; v. 찔러 넣다; 고수하다; 꼼짝하지 않다
A stick is a thin branch which has fallen off a tree.

peel [pi:l] n. (과일·채소 등의) 껍질; v. 껍질을 벗기다; 벗겨지다; 떨어져 나가다
The peel of a fruit such as a lemon or an apple is its skin.

aside [əsáid] ad. 한쪽으로; (길을) 비켜; (나중에 쓰려고) 따로
If you move something aside, you move it to one side of you.

awful [ɔ́:fəl] a. 끔찍한, 지독한; 엄청
If you say that something is awful, you mean that it is extremely unpleasant, shocking, or bad.

breath [breθ] n. 숨, 입김 (hold one's breath idiom 숨을 멈추다; 숨을 죽이다)
If you hold your breath, you make yourself stop breathing for a few moments.

settle for idiom (꼭 원하는 것은 아니지만) ~에 만족하다
If you settle for something, you accept something that is not quite what you wanted but is the best that you can get.

faint [feint] v. 실신하다, 기절하다; a. 희미한, 약한; 어지러운
If you faint, you lose consciousness for a short time, especially because you are hungry, or because of pain, heat, or shock.

bend [bend] v. (bent–bent) 굽히다, 숙이다; 구부리다; n. 굽이, 굽은 곳
When you bend, you move the top part of your body downward and forward.

crumple [krʌmpl] v. 구기다, 구겨지다; (얼굴이) 일그러지다
(crumpled a. 구겨진, 쭈글쭈글한)
If you crumple something such as paper or cloth, or if it crumples, it is squashed and becomes full of untidy creases and folds.

overnight [òuvərnáit] ad. 밤사이에, 하룻밤 동안; a. 하룻밤 사이의, 갑작스러운
If something happens overnight, it happens throughout the night or at some point during the night.

ride [raid] v. (차량·자전거·말 등을) 타다; n. (차량·자전거 등을) 타고 달리기; 여정
When you ride a bicycle or a motorcycle, you sit on it, control it, and travel along on it.

uphill [ʌphíl] ad. 오르막길로, 언덕 위로; a. 오르막의
If something or someone is uphill or is moving uphill, they are near the top of a hill or are going up a slope.

respect [rispékt] n. 존경(심), 경의; 존중, 정중; v. 존경하다; 존중하다
If you have respect for someone, you have a good opinion of them.

shrug [ʃrʌg] v. (어깨를) 으쓱하다; n. (어깨를) 으쓱하기
If you shrug, you raise your shoulders to show that you are not interested in something or that you do not know or care about something.

rag [ræg] n. 해진 천, 누더기
A rag is a piece of old cloth which you can use to clean or wipe things.

wipe [waip] v. (먼지·물기 등을) 닦다; 지우다; n. 닦기, 훔치기
If you wipe something, you rub its surface to remove dirt or liquid from it.

grin [grin] v. 활짝 웃다; n. 활짝 웃음
When you grin, you smile broadly.

broad [brɔːd] a. 넓은; 광대한; 일반적인 (**broadly** ad. 활짝; 대략)
A broad smile is one in which your mouth is stretched very wide because you are very pleased or amused.

Chapter 10

1. **Why did Catherine have to be outside with her family?**

   A. They were moving to a new apartment.

   B. They were having a bike race.

   C. It was a beautiful day.

   D. It was a family moment.

2. **How long had Francine and her father worked on the bike?**

   A. A day

   B. A week

   C. A month

   D. A year

3. Which of the following was NOT true about Francine's restored bike?

A. The banana seat had been polished.

B. It had racing stripes on the fenders.

C. It had more gears.

D. It was still purple.

4. Why did Francine's father take the bike for its first test drive?

A. Francine wanted him to make sure it was safe to ride.

B. He wanted to have the honors of the first ride.

C. He wanted to relive his childhood glory.

D. Francine wanted him to ride first.

5. What happened after Francine's father turned around the corner out of sight?

A. He made sure that it was safe to ride.

B. He got off of the bike and walked it back home.

C. He pushed off fast and went down the street.

D. He saw some children who laughed at him.

1분에 몇 단어를 읽는지 리딩 속도를 측정해보세요.

$$\frac{416 \ words}{reading \ time \ (\quad) \ sec} \times 60 = (\quad) \ WPM$$

Build Your Vocabulary

afraid [əfréid] a. 걱정하는; 두려워하는, 겁내는
If you are afraid that something unpleasant will happen, you are worried that it may happen and you want to avoid it.

mutter [mʌtər] v. 투덜거리다; 중얼거리다; n. 중얼거림
If you mutter, you speak very quietly so that you cannot easily be heard, often because you are complaining about something.

sheet [ʃiːt] n. 시트, 얇은 천; (종이) 한 장 (bed sheet n. 침대에 까는 천)
A sheet is a large rectangular piece of cotton or other cloth that you sleep on or cover yourself with in a bed.

drape [dreip] v. (느슨하게) 걸치다, 씌우다; 가리다; 장식하다; n. 휘장
If someone or something is draped in a piece of cloth, they are loosely covered by it.

work on idiom (해결하기 위해) ~에 애쓰다; (원하는) 효과가 나다
If you work on something, you practice or work hard in order to improve it.

present [prizént] ① v. 소개하다; 주다, 수여하다; n. 선물 ② a. 현재의; 있는; n. 현재
If you present someone to someone else, often an important person, you formally introduce them.

improve [imprúːv] v. 개선되다, 나아지다; 향상시키다 (improved a. 향상된, 개선된)
If something improves or if you improve it, it gets better.

restore [ristɔ́:r] v. 복원하다, 복구하다; 회복시키다
When someone restores something, they repair and clean it, so that it looks like it did when it was new.

clap [klæp] v. 박수를 치다; 손뼉을 치다; n. 박수, 손뼉
When you clap, you hit your hands together to show appreciation or attract attention.

bright [brait] a. 선명한, 밝은; 눈부신, 빛나는; 똑똑한 (**brightly** ad. 선명하게, 밝게)
A bright color is strong and noticeable, and not dark.

gleam [gli:m] v. (아주 깨끗하게) 반짝이다; 희미하게 빛나다; (눈빛이) 반짝거리다; n. 어슴푸레한 빛; (눈의) 번득거림
If an object or a surface gleams, it reflects light because it is shiny and clean.

rub [rʌb] v. 문지르다, 비비다; (두 손 등을) 맞비비다; n. 문지르기, 비비기
If you rub an object or a surface, you move a cloth backward and forward over it in order to clean or dry it.

polish [páliʃ] v. 닦다, 광을 내다; 다듬다; n. 닦기; 윤, 광택
If you polish something, you put polish on it or rub it with a cloth to make it shine.

luster [lʌ́stər] n. 광택, 윤; 광채, 빛남; v. 광내다, 갈고 닦다; 빛나다
Luster is gentle shining light that is reflected from a surface, for example from polished metal.

beam [bi:m] v. 활짝 웃다; 비추다; n. 빛줄기; 환한 미소
If you say that someone is beaming, you mean that they have a big smile on their face because they are happy or proud about something.

confess [kənfés] v. 고백하다, 인정하다; (죄·잘못을) 자백하다
You use expressions like 'I confess' or 'I have to confess' to apologize slightly for admitting something you are ashamed of or that you think might offend or annoy someone.

touch [tʌtʃ] n. (마무리) 손질; 마무리; 만지기, 손길; v. 만지다; 닿다, 접촉하다
A touch is a detail which is added to something to improve it.

race [reis] v. 경주하다, 경쟁하다; 쏜살같이 가다; n. 경주; 인종, 민족
If you race, you take part in a race.

stripe [straip] n. 줄무늬
A stripe is a long line which is a different color from the areas next to it.

admit [ædmít] v. 인정하다, 시인하다
If you admit that something bad, unpleasant, or embarrassing is true, you agree, often unwillingly, that it is true.

in fact idiom 사실은, 실은; 실제로는
You use 'in fact' to indicate that you are giving more detailed information about what you have just said.

nail [neil] n. 손톱; 못; v. 못으로 박다
Your nails are the thin hard parts that grow at the ends of your fingers and toes.

praise [preiz] n. 칭찬, 찬사, 찬양; v. 칭찬하다; 찬송하다
Praise is what you say that expresses your admiration and approval of someone or something.

pause [pɔːz] v. (말·일을 하다가) 잠시 멈추다; 정지시키다; n. 멈춤
If you pause while you are doing something, you stop for a short period and then continue.

test drive [tést draiv] n. 시운전; 시승; v. 시운전하다
A test drive is an act of driving a motor vehicle that you are considering buying, in order to determine its quality.

honor [ánər] n. 영광, 특권; 명예; 존경; v. 존경하다, 공경하다; 명예를 주다
If someone does the honors at a social occasion or public event, they act as host or perform some official function.

bow [bau] v. (허리를 굽혀) 절하다; (고개를) 숙이다; n. 절, (고개 숙여 하는) 인사
When you bow to someone, you briefly bend your body toward them as a formal way of greeting them or showing respect.

aside [əsáid] ad. 한쪽으로; (길을) 비켜; (나중에 쓰려고) 따로
If you move something aside, you move it to one side of you.

deprive [dipráiv] v. 빼앗다, 허용치 않다, 주지 않다; 박탈하다
If you deprive someone of something that they want or need, you take it away from them, or you prevent them from having it.

strap [stræp] v. 끈으로 묶다; 붕대를 감다; n. 끈, 줄, 띠
If you strap something somewhere, you fasten it there with a narrow piece of leather or cloth.

wave aside idiom ～을 물리치다, 일축하다
To wave something aside means to ignore someone's ideas, feelings, or opinions because you do not think they are important.

ride [raid] v. (차량·자전거·말 등을) 타다; n. (차량·자전거 등을) 타고 달리기; 여정
When you ride a bicycle or a motorcycle, you sit on it, control it, and travel along on it.

spin [spin] v. (휙) 돌아서다; 돌리다, 회전시키다; n. 회전, 돌기
If something spins or if you spin it, it turns quickly around a central point.

block [blak] n. 구역, 블록; 사각형 덩어리; v. 막다, 차단하다; 방해하다
A block in a town is an area of land with streets on all its sides.

absolute [ǽbsəlùːt] a. 완전한, 완벽한; 확실한 (absolutely ad. 전적으로, 틀림없이)
Absolutely means totally and completely.

mount [maunt] v. (자전거·말 등에) 올라타다; 고정시키다; n. 오르기; (말 등을) 타기
If you mount a horse or bicycle, you climb on to it so that you can ride it.

wobble [wabl] v. (불안하게) 뒤뚱거리며 가다; 흔들리다, 떨리다; n. 흔들림, 떨림
If something or someone wobbles, they make small movements from side to side, for example because they are unsteady.

sidewalk [sáidwɔ:k] n. (포장한) 보도, 인도
A sidewalk is a path with a hard surface by the side of a road.

sight [sait] n. 시야; 광경, 모습; 시력; v. 갑자기 보다, 찾다
(out of sight idiom 보이지 않는 곳에)
If something is out of sight, you cannot see it.

push off idiom 멀어져 가다, 떠나가다
If you push off, you leave someone or a place.

whiz [hwiz] v. 쌩 하고 지나가다; n. 윙, 핑 (하고 빠르게 움직이는 소리)
If something whizzes somewhere, it moves there very fast.

light up idiom (두 눈·얼굴이) 환해지다; 환하게 되다
If a person's eyes or face light up, or something lights them up, they become bright with excitement or happiness.

glee [gli:] n. 신이 남; 큰 기쁨, 환희
Glee is a feeling of happiness and excitement.

disappear [disəpíər] v. 사라지다, 보이지 않게 되다; 실종되다, 없어지다
If you say that someone or something disappears, you mean that you can no longer see them, usually because you or they have changed position.

experience [ikspíəriəns] n. 일, 체험, 경험; v. 겪다, 경험하다; 느끼다
Experience is used to refer to the past events, knowledge, and feelings that make up someone's life or character.

count on idiom ~을 믿다; ~을 확신하다
If you count on someone, you depend on them to do what you want or expect them to do for you.

1장

page 5

프렌스키 가족은 그들의 아파트에서 저녁을 먹고 있었습니다. 적어도 프렌스키 씨와 프렌스키 부인 그리고 그들의 큰딸, 캐서린은 저녁을 먹고 있었습니다. 그들의 작은딸, 프랜신은 아무것도 먹고 있지 않았습니다. 그녀는 팔짱을 낀 채로 의자에 앉아있기만 했습니다.

"프랜신이 부루퉁해 하고 있어요." 캐서린이 말했습니다.

"아니야." 프랜신이 말했습니다. "난 그게 무슨 뜻인지도 몰라."

"그 의미는 네가 조금, 음, 기분이 언짢다는 거란다." 그녀의 아버지, 올리버가 말했습니다. "네 뜻대로 되지 않아서 조금 화가 나 있다는 뜻이지."

page 6

"음, 제가 왜 그렇지 않겠어요?" 프랜신이 말했습니다.

"미안하구나, 애야." 그녀의 엄마, 라번이 말했습니다. "하지만 우리는 지금 당장 네게 새 자전거를 사줄 여유가 없구나. 어쩌면 내년에는..."

프랜신은 계속 퉁퉁거렸습니다. "이건 불공평해요. 자전거가 없다면 저는 그냥 죽어버릴 거예요."

그녀의 아버지는 헉 하고 숨을 쉬었습니다. "안 돼, 그게 사실이 아니라고 말하렴!" 그는 한쪽 무릎을 꿇고 프랜신의 손을 잡았습니다. "포기하면 안 된다, 애야. 살아야 해, 다시 말하건대, 살아야 한단다!"

그는 계속할 수도 있었지만, 프랜신이 키득거리기 시작했습니다. 곧바로 그 자신도 웃고 있었습니다.

"오, 아빠." 캐서린이 말했습니다. "아빠는 정말 그런 바보 같은 장난이 효과가 있을 거라고 생각하시는 거예요?"

그녀의 아버지는 그녀에게 경례했고 똑바로 일어섰습니다. "글쎄, 네가 프랜신 나이였을 때 너에게 효과가 있었단다." 그는 턱을 쓰다듬었습니다. "하지만 아마 네가 맞을지도 몰라. 나도 내가 어쩌다 그랬는지 모르겠구나. 게다가, 내게 좋은 생각이 있단다."

page 7

그는 테이블에서 일어나서 프랜신에게 자신의 손을 내밀었습니다. "나랑 같이 가자꾸나." 그가 말했습니다.

그들은 프렌스키 가족의 창고가 있는 지하로 내려갔습니다. 그녀의 아버지가 그것을 여는 동안, 프랜신은 맨 아래 계단에 앉았습니다. 그녀는 여기까지 내려온 이유가 무엇인지 알 수 없었습니다. 그곳은 어두웠고, 거미줄이 드리워져 있었으며, 조금 이상한 냄새가 났습니다.

"손전등을 이쪽으로 비추럼." 그녀의

아버지가 말했습니다.

프랜신은 구석으로 빛을 비췄습니다. "이제 좀 낫구나." 프렌스키 씨는 상자들 뒤를 뒤졌습니다. "아하! 여기 있구나!"

그가 상자를 옆으로 밀어 한 대의 낡은 자전거를 드러냈습니다. 그리고는 그가 그것을 굴려서 그녀에게 가져왔습니다.

"북소리를 부탁해요!"

프랜신의 얼굴이 시무룩해졌습니다. 이 자전거는 단지 낡기만 한 것이 아니었습니다. 그것은 보기 싫기도 했습니다. 페인트가 벗겨진 밝은 보라색, 녹슨 손잡이, 그리고 반짝거리는 어두운 주황색의 바나나 모양 안장까지.

"이게 *뭐예요*?" 그녀가 물었습니다.

"너의 새 자전거란다." 그녀의 아버지가 설명했습니다. "뭐, 사실 이건 오래된 새 자전거지." 그는 손잡이 사이의 엄청난 거미줄을 걷어내었습니다.

"아빠, 석기 시대 이래로 자전거는 꽤 많이 바뀌었다고요."

그녀의 아버지는 그것을 살펴보았습니다. "난 잘 모르겠구나. 자전거는 여전히 바퀴 두 개, 안장, 그리고 손잡이가 달렸지. 그리고 이런 바나나 모양 안장은 흔히 볼 수 있는 게 아니란다. 확실히 수집가용 물건이지."

"하지만 저는 수집가용 물건은 원하지 않아요. 저는 21단 기어가 달린 크로스 자전거를 원한다고요."

page 10

그녀의 아버지가 웃었습니다. "그 모든 기어들은 헷갈리기만 하지. 3단 기어면 충분하단다." 그는 딸깍거리는 소리를 내며 기어를 바꾸면서 바퀴를 돌렸습니다. "이것이 필요한 건 단지 약간의 기름뿐이란다. 이건 상태가 좋잖아. 내가 네 나이였을 때, 난 매일 이걸 타고 학교에 갔지. 난 네가 나만큼이나 이걸 좋아하게 될 거라고 생각한단다."

그는 행복하게 안장을 토닥거렸습니다.

프랜신은 그저 한숨을 쉬었습니다. "하는 수 없네요." 그녀가 말했습니다.

그러나 그녀에게는 별로 희망이 없었습니다.

2장

page 11

"그건 자전거가 아니야." 아서가 말하고 있었습니다. "자전거는 날 수 없다고."

"음, 그건 맞아." 버스터가 인정했습니다. 그들은 *바이오닉 버니* 프로그램의 어젯밤 방송에 대해 이야기하고 있었습니다. 버니에게는 악당과 온갖 나쁜 녀

석들을 쫓을 새로운 이동수단이 생겼습니다.

"난 그 프로그램을 전혀 보지 않아." 머피가 자신의 자전거를 채우며 말했습니다. "봐야 할 훨씬 더 교육적이고 중요한 것이 있다고."

"예를 들면 어떤 것?" 버스터와 아서가 함께 말했습니다.

"홈쇼핑 채널이지, 물론. 만약 네가 거기에 주의를 기울이지 않는다면, 넌 아주 훌륭한 구매 기회를 놓칠 수 있단 말이야."

page 12

버스터가 자신의 눈을 굴렸습니다. "난 내 운에 맡기겠어." 그가 말했습니다.

"무엇을 운에 맡긴다는 거니?" 프랜신이 그들의 뒤로 자전거를 타고 왔고 그녀의 자전거에서 내리면서 물었습니다.

버스터가 그녀를 향해 몸을 돌렸습니다. "홈쇼핑 채널을 건너뛰는 걸로—" 그는 말을 멈추고 가만히 바라보았습니다. "네가 타고 있는 건 뭐니?"

다른 아이들도 보았습니다.

"우와!"

"내 선글라스가 어디 있지?"

"하, 하." 프랜신이 말했습니다. "이건 내 새로운 자전거야."

버스터가 웃었습니다. "새로운 거라고? 몇 세기에 말이야?"

"내 자전거와 같은 것을 사지 못해서 참 안됐다." 머피가 말했습니다. 그녀는 최신 모델: 24단 기어, 그라파이트 합금 뼈대, 그리고 방사성 패턴의 브레이크 패드를 갖춘 자전거를 갖고 있었습니다.

page 14

"난 내가 원하는 어떤 자전거도 가질 수 있었어." 프랜신이 말했습니다. "하지만 난 이것을 선택했어."

머피가 얼굴을 찡그렸습니다. "하지만 프랜신… 왜?"

"음, 전통 때문에. 이 자전거는 아빠 것이었거든. 마치 집안의 가보 같은 거야. 그는 이걸로 온갖 묘기를 부릴 수 있었어."

"내 생각엔 그게 이걸 특별하게 하는 것 같긴 하네." 머피가 인정했습니다. 그렇지만 그녀는 그다지 납득하지 않은 것처럼 보였습니다.

"가장 엄청난 묘기는 말이야." 버스터가 아서에게 속삭였습니다. "그녀가 이 자전거를 조금이라도 더 좋아 보이게 할 수 있을지의 여부야."

그날 오후 늦게, 아이들의 선생님인, 랫번 선생님이 학급 학생들에게 슬라이드를 보여주고 있었습니다.

"바퀴는." 그가 말했습니다. "약 오천 년 전에 중동에서 발명되었던 것으로 여겨진단다."

"수메르 사람들에 의해서인가요 아니면 바빌로니아 사람들에 의해서인가요?" 브레인이 물었습니다.

"난 항상 그 모든 *어디 사람들*이란 게 헷갈려." 아서가 한숨을 쉬었습니다.

"그건 혼란스럽지." 랫번 선생님이 동의했습니다. "이 경우엔 내 생각에는 수메르 사람들인 것 같구나. 이 고대 사람들이 그들의 새로운 바퀴로 무엇을 했는지 누가 말해줄 수 있니?"

버스터가 자기 팔을 힘차게 흔들었습니다.

"그래, 버스터?"

"프랜신의 자전거를 만들었죠."

모두 웃었습니다—프랜신과 머피를 제외한 모두 말입니다. 심지어 랫번 선생님이 그들에게 멈추라고 말한 후에도, 몇몇 아이들은 계속해서 낄낄 웃었습니다.

"프랜신을 그만 괴롭혀." 머피가 버스터에게 말했습니다.

"맞아!" 프랜신이 말했습니다.

"그녀가 흉하고 낡은 자전거를 타야만 하는 건 그녀의 잘못이 아니라고." 머피가 계속 말했습니다.

프랜신이 눈을 깜박거렸습니다. "오?"

머피가 자신의 손가락으로 버스터의 가슴을 찔렀습니다. "네가 어떻게 느낄지 한번 생각해보란 말이야." 그녀가 말했습니다.

버스터의 얼굴이 웃던 중에 바뀌었습니다. 그는 부끄러워하는 것처럼 보였습니다. 다른 모든 사람들도 마찬가지였습니다. 그들은 매우 조용해졌습니다.

그렇지만 그들 누구도 프랜신이 아무도 볼 수 없는 마음속 깊이 느끼는 것만큼 부끄럽지는 않았습니다.

3장

학교가 끝난 후, 모두 여전히 복도에서 이야기를 하는 동안에 프랜신은 밖으로 급히 뛰쳐나갔습니다. 그녀는 화가 나는 동시에 슬프기도 했습니다. 이 새 자전거는 계속 문제만 일으키고 있었습니다. 그것은 모든 사람이 그녀를 다르게 보도록 하고 있었습니다. 그녀는 무언가 특별한 일로 눈에 띄는 것은 개의치 않았습니다—훌륭한 속구를 던지는 것 같은 일로 말입니다. 그러나 놀림 당하고 웃음거리가 되는 것은 재미있지 않았습니다. 하나도 재미있지 않았습니다.

그녀는 곧장 자전거 거치대로 가며, 반쯤은 이 모든 게 나쁜 꿈이었으면 좋겠다고 바랐습니다.

그러나 그건 꿈이 아니었습니다. 그리고 그녀의 자전거는 바뀌지 않았습니다. 그것은 그 역겨운 자줏빛의 찬란함을 뽐내며, 그곳에 여전히 서 있었습니다.

왜 누가 여기에 와서 이걸 훔쳐가진 않는 걸까? 그녀는 궁금했습니다. 그들에게는 온종일 시간이 있었는데 말이죠.

뭐, 아무도 이 자전거를 가져가지 않았지만, 그건 그녀가 계속 그것을 바라보고 있어야 한다는 뜻은 아니었습니다. 주위를 힐끔 둘러보자, 그녀는 학교 운동장 가장자리에 있는 수풀을 발견했습니다. 그녀는 그 수풀로 자전거를 굴려서 끌고 갔고 그것을 쓰레기통 뒤에 기대어 놓았습니다.

잠시, 그녀는 자전거가 그녀에게 슬픈 표정을 짓고 있다고 생각했습니다.

"걱정하지 마." 그녀가 속삭였습니다. "난 너를 버리는 게 아니야. 어쨌든, 아직은 아니야. 난 그저 조금 생각할 시간이 필요해. 그리고 내가 생각할 동안에는 너를 보지 않는 편이 나아."

그리고는 그녀는 학교 정문으로 뛰어 돌아갔습니다.

아서, 머피 그리고 버스터가 그녀를 기다리고 있었습니다. 그들은 모두 자신들의 자전거와 배낭을 갖고 있었습니다.

"너 어디 있었니?" 머피가 물었습니다. "너는 교실에서 엄청 빠르게 사라졌잖아."

아서가 버스터의 옆구리를 찔렀습니다. "버스터가 너에게 무언가 말하고 싶은 게 있대, 안 그래, 버스터?"

"음, 맞아, 있어." 버스터가 말했습니다. 그는 목을 가다듬었습니다. "프랜신, 내가 아까 말했던 거 미안해. 네 자전거를 모욕한 거 말이야, 내 말은."

"그리고 우리도 웃어서 미안해." 아서가 말했습니다. "있잖아, 우리 아빠는 초창기에 요리할 때 쓰시던 낡아빠진 프라이팬을 갖고 있어. 그건 온통 새까맣고, 찌그러지고 긁힌 자국도 있지. 내가 한번은 아빠께 왜 대신 사용할 반짝거리는 새것을 사지 않으시냐고 여쭤본 적이 있어. 아빠는 오래된 팬에는 친숙한 무언가가 있어서 음식을 더 맛있게 해준다고 말씀하셨어. 분명 너의 자전거도 네 아버지에게는 그럴 것 같아."

프랜신은 고개를 끄덕였습니다. 그녀는 기분이 조금 나아졌습니다. "고마워, 아서." 그녀가 말했습니다. "그리고 너도, 버스터."

머피는 자전거 거치대를 훑어보았습니다. "그런데, 네 자전거는 어디 있니?"

그녀가 물었습니다.

"오, 음, 난 지금 이 순간에는 그것을 타지 않으려고.... 난 그냥 조금 걷고 싶네."

"우리는 슈가 볼에 갈 거야." 아서가 말했습니다. "너도 올래?"

프랜신은 별로 그럴 기분이 아니었습니다. 비록 친구들이 사과해서 기쁘긴 했지만, 그녀는 여전히 어울리지 못하는 기분이었습니다. 왜 그녀가 두드러지는 사람이 되어야만 하는 걸까요? 그녀는 사람들이 그녀를 안타까워하는 것을 원하지 않았습니다—설령 그들이 그것에 대해 다정하게 굴어도 말입니다.

"난 다음에 같이 갈게." 그녀가 말했습니다.

아서가 어깨를 들썩했습니다. "알았어."

"잘 가." 머피와 버스터가 말했습니다.

그들 모두 자전거를 타고, 생각에 잠긴 프랜신을 두고 갔습니다.

4장

page 22

그날 밤에 프랜신은 침대 가장자리에 앉아서, 바닥에 테니스공을 튕기고 있었습니다.

탕. 탕. 탕. 탕.

튕길 때마다, 프랜신은 새로운 자전거가 생기기를 바랐습니다. 그리고 그냥 아무 자전거가 아니었습니다. 아서와 버스터가 자신들도 갖기를 원할 만한 자전거였습니다. 머피마저도 감탄할 법한 자전거 말입니다.

그녀의 아버지가 불쑥 들어왔습니다. "이게 무슨 소리니? 아, 너는 신체 조정력 훈련을 하고 있구나, 응?"

"그런 것 같아요."

page 23

"훈련은 중요한 거란다. 너의 야구 코치로서, 난 그것을 단언할 수 있지. 그리고 조정력에 대해서 말이 나와서 말인데, 새로운 자전거는 어떠니? 안장 높이는 알맞니?"

"자전거가 보라색이죠." 프랜신이 무심하게 말했습니다. "정말 보라색이에요."

그녀의 아버지가 고개를 끄덕였습니다. "그게 내가 네 나이였을 때 가장 좋아하던 색이란다. 있지, 보라색은 왕족의 색이야. 위엄 있고. 장엄하지."

"정말요?" 프랜신이 말했습니다.

"응, 그럼. 고대에는 아주 가치 있게 여겨졌단다."

"그러니까 사람들이 바퀴를 발명하던 오래전 그때를 말씀하시는 건가요?"

"그렇지."

프랜신이 한숨지었습니다. "그럴 줄

알았어요." 그녀가 말했습니다.

"그러니 자연스럽게 자전거의 색깔로 고르기에 훌륭하다고 여겼지."

프렌스키 씨가 자신의 얼굴로 이상한 표정을 지었습니다. 프랜신은 그것을 전에 본 적이 있었습니다. 그것은 그의 소년시절을 추억하는 표정이었습니다. 이야기가 뒤따르기 마련이었습니다.

page 24

"그거 정말 잘 달리지 않니? 그것이 얼마나 모퉁이를 잘 도는지 느꼈어? 난 우리가 동네를 가로질러서 경주하려고 했던 게 기억이 난단다. 내 오래된 자전거로는 아빠는 우승 근처에도 가지 못했었지. 그때 내가 이걸 갖게 되었어."

프랜신이 공을 튀기던 것을 멈추었습니다. "어떻게 됐나요?" 그녀가 물었습니다.

"음, 우리는 모두 나란히 줄을 섰지. 그리고 한 아이가 있었어, 덩치가 큰 아이로, 자기 자전거가 얼마나 빠른지 늘 우쭐대던 아이였지. 어떤 유형의 아이인지 알잖니. 나는 그 애를 몹시 이기고 싶었단다."

프랜신이 고개를 끄덕였습니다.

"그렇게 경주가 시작됐고, 나는 미친 듯이 페달을 밟았지. 그리고 바나나 모양의 안장이 있어서, 나는 정말 힘껏 페달을 디딜 수 있었어. 난 내가 그들을 추월할 때 몇몇 아이들의 얼굴에 떠오른 표정을 절대 잊을 수가 없단다."

"그래서 이기셨나요?"

page 26

그녀의 아버지가 웃었습니다. "그렇지도 않았지. 그 덩치 큰 아이가 이겼단다—늘 그랬듯이. 그렇지만 적어도 나는 딱 중간은 갔단다. 나에겐 그게 큰 발전이었지."

"오."

아버지는 그녀를 바라보았습니다. "그렇게 실망스러운 표정을 짓지 말렴, 프랜신. 나는 더 잘할 수 있다는 것만으로도 매우 행복했단다."

"그게 아니에요. 제가 궁금했던 것은..."

"응?"

"음, 아빠는 막 이 새로운 자전거를 갖게 된 것이 아빠에게 얼마나 신나는 일이었는지에 대해 말씀하셨잖아요."

"그렇고말고. 난 내가 너무 크게 미소 짓고 있어서 얼굴이 찢어지는 줄 알았어."

"그런데 모르시겠어요? 그 당시에는 그것이 아빠에게 새로운 것이었죠. 저에게는 더는 새로운 것이 아니에요. 제가 새로운 자전거를 산다면, 저는 아마 아빠가 그랬던 것처럼 똑같이 느낄 거예요."

프렌스키 씨는 한숨지었습니다. "내가 너에게 새로운 걸로 사줄 수 있으면

좋겠구나, 얘야. 하지만 우리는 지금 여 윳돈이 없단다. 그리고 내 오래된 자전 거는 길고 자랑스러운 역사를 가지고 있지. 유감스럽지만 지금은 네가 그걸로 만족해야 할 것 같구나."

page27

프랜신은 다시 공을 튀기기 시작했 습니다. 그녀는 만족하는 것과는 거리 가 멀었습니다. 아주 멀리 말입니다. 그 리고 아버지가 말씀하시는 투를 보아서 는, 그녀는 자신이 당분간 만족하지 못 할 것임을 알 수 있었습니다.

5장

page 28

다음 날 아침, 프랜신은 학교로 천천히 걸어갔습니다. 그녀는 새로운 날의 시작 이 그녀의 기분을 더 나아지게 해주기 를 바랐습니다. 하지만 해가 빛나고 새 들이 노래하고 있어도, 그녀는 그 전날 만큼이나 기분이 좋지 않았습니다.

그녀가 모퉁이를 돌았을 때, 저 앞에 서 그녀는 자신이 자전거를 숨겨두었던 수풀을 보았습니다. 하지만, 그녀의 시 야는 쓰레기 트럭에 어느 정도 가려져 있었습니다. 쓰레기를 수거하는 사람들 이 일찍 나와서, 쓰레기통을 비우고 있 었습니다.

"오, 이런!" 그녀가 생각했습니다.

바로 그때, 그 남자들 가운데 한 사람 이 프랜신의 자전거를 집어 들었고 트럭 안으로 던져버렸습니다.

page 29

프랜신은 뛰기 시작했습니다.

"이봐요! 저기요!" 그녀가 팔을 흔들 며, 소리쳤습니다. "돌아와요! 당신은 거 기에 내 자전거를 갖고 있다고요!"

하지만 수거하는 사람들은 트럭의 엔 진에서 나는 굉음 때문에 그녀가 말하 는 것을 들을 수 없었습니다. 그녀가 그 들의 주의를 끌기 전에 그들은 떠나가 버렸습니다.

프랜신은 멈추었습니다. 그녀는 가쁘 게 숨을 쉬고 있었습니다. 이것은 끔찍 했습니다! 자전거는 없어졌습니다. 그녀 는 이제 어떻게 해야 하는 걸까요? 그녀 는 자신의 아버지가 뭐라고 말할지 상 상할 수 있었습니다.

그녀가 학교 운동장으로 들어갈 때, 버스터와 아서가 자신들의 자전거를 타 고 빠르게 달려왔습니다. 아서가 브레이 크를 밟아 멈춰 서는 동안 버스터는 그 들 주위를 빙빙 돌았습니다.

"안녕, 프랜신!" 버스터가 말했습니 다. "수업이 시작되기 전에 앞바퀴 들고 자전거 타기 좀 할래?"

"난 할 수 없어." 프랜신이 말했습니 다. "내 자전거가 없어."

"어디에 있는데?" 아서가 물었습니다.

"잘 모르겠어." 그녀가 말했습니다. 비록 그녀는 자전거를 없애서 한편으로는 좋기도 했지만, 그녀는 자신의 친구들에게 무슨 일이 일어났는지 말하는 것이 편치는 않았습니다.

"어떻게 모를 수가 있어?" 버스터가 물었습니다. 그도 가끔 자기 물건을 잃어버리곤 했지만, 자전거처럼 큰 것은 아니었습니다.

갑자기 프랜신에게 좋은 생각이 났습니다. "내, 음, 자전거를 도둑맞았어."

"도둑맞았다고!" 아서가 말했습니다. "너 확실해?"

"물론 확실하겠지." 버스터가 말했습니다. "보통 그런 것을 가지고서 실수하지는 않잖아. 그렇지, 프랜신?"

"음, 그래. 내 말은, 나는 어제는 그것을 갖고 있었어." 그녀가 잠시 말을 멈췄습니다. "그리고 지금은 그게 사라졌어."

"사라졌다고? 무엇이 사라졌는데?" 머피와 함께 막 도착한, 수 엘렌이 말했습니다.

"누군가가 프랜신의 자전거를 훔쳤어." 아서가 말했습니다.

"그거 끔찍하구나." 수 엘렌이 말했습니다.

머피는 혼란스러워 보였습니다. "도대체 누가 훔치겠어, 그런—내 말은, 네 자전거를?" 그녀가 물었습니다.

프랜신은 어깨를 들썩였습니다. "그건 꽤 낡긴 했지…"

머피가 헉 하고 숨 쉬었습니다. "얘, 어쩌면 그게 이유일 수도 있겠어! 만약 그것이 정말 오래되어서 골동품이라면?" 그녀가 팔을 휘젓기 시작했습니다. "경찰관님! 도와주세요!"

"무슨 일이니?" 그들 뒤에서 다가오며, 브레인이 물었습니다

"프랜신의 자전거를 도둑맞았어." 버스터가 말했습니다. "내가 확신하는데 그건 아마 국제 자전거 도둑 조직의 짓이었을 거야. 그들은 아마 그것을 암시장에 내다 팔 거야."

"아니, 아니야." 자전거를 도둑맞았다고 말한 것이 전혀 좋은 생각이 아니었다고 생각하기 시작한, 프랜신이 말했습니다.

"진정해." 아서가 말했습니다. "허둥대지 말자."

"우리는 하니 교장 선생님께 말해야 해." 브레인이 말했습니다.

"네 말이 맞아." 아서가 말했습니다. "아마 우리는 아직 그것을 훔친 사람을 잡을 수 있을 거야. 그들은 그렇게 멀리 가지는 못했을 거야."

page 33

"아니야! 잠깐만!" 프랜신이 말했습니다. 그녀는 이 일에 학교 교장 선생님을 끌어들이고 싶지 않았습니다. 하지만 이미 늦은 후였습니다. 모든 다른 아이들이 학교로 뛰어가고 있었습니다.

그녀가 할 수 있는 것이라고는 그들의 뒤를 따라가는 것뿐이었습니다.

6장

page 34

하니 교장 선생님이 자신의 책상 뒤에서 프랜신을 지그시 쳐다보았습니다.

"이것을 확실히 하자." 그가 말했습니다. "너는 집안일을 하기 위해서 어제 자전거를 타고 집에 급하게 가고 있었다고."

프랜신이 고개를 끄덕였습니다.

"그리고 그 집안일이란 것이 뭐지?"

프랜신은 잠시 생각했습니다. "오, 있잖아요, 제 방을 청소하기, 저녁 식사를 만드는 것을 돕기 같은 것들이요."

"와, 나는 감동받았어." 브레인이 버스터에게 속삭였습니다. "난 집안일을 하려고 절대 집에 급하게 가지 않는데." 그들은 아서와 머피와 함께 프랜신 뒤에 서 있었습니다.

page 35

하니 교장선생님은 자신의 턱을 긁적였습니다. "그리고 너는 급히 갔다고 했지, 맞지?"

"맞아요."

프렌신은 행복하게 휘파람 불면서, 자전거를 타고 가고 있는 자신의 모습을 볼 수 있었습니다. 갑자기 커다란 트럭이 그녀의 뒤로 다가왔습니다. 그것은 마치 쓰레기 트럭 같았지만, 뒤에 커다란 갈고리가 달려 있었습니다.

그 갈고리가 아래로 내려왔고 프랜신의 자전거를 잡았습니다. 갈고리가 자전거를 들어 올렸고 그것을 트럭에 떨어뜨리기 전에 그녀는 간신히 뛰어내릴 수 있었습니다.

그리고 나서 그 트럭은 그것을 향해 주먹을 흔드는 프랜신을 남겨 둔 채, 속도를 높여 떠나갔습니다.

"네가 그 자동차 번호를 알아내진 않은 것 같네." 브레인이 말했습니다.

"미안." 프랜신이 말했습니다. "난 내가 살아서 탈출한 것만으로도 다행이라고 생각했는걸."

하니 교장 선생님은 걱정하는 것처럼 보이려고 애썼습니다. "나는 그런 트럭들이 길거리를 돌아다니는지 전혀 몰랐구나. 커다란 갈고리, 그렇게 말했지? 난 이걸 누군가에게 보고해야겠구나."

page 37

"APB를 발표해야 해요!" 버스터가 말했습니다.

"APB?" 머피가 말했다.

"전국 지명 수배라는 거야." 아서가 설명했습니다.

버스터가 고개를 끄덕였습니다. "주립 경찰관들이 고속도로를 뒤덮어야만 해요. 그들은 모든 휴게소를 다 뒤져봐야 한다고요."

버스터가 하는 말을 들으면서, 프랜신은 자신의 기분이 점점 더 불편해지는 것을 느꼈습니다. "음, 하니 교장 선생님... 아직 하루가 시작되지 않았다는 걸 알지만, 저 집에 가도 될까요? 저는 몸이 조금 안 좋네요."

"너는 정말 조금 창백해 보이는구나." 하니 교장선생님이 말했습니다. "간호사가 너를 한번 살펴보도록 해야겠구나. 그녀가 동의한다면, 누구에게 전화해서 널 데리러 오라고 하면 되겠니?"

프랜신은 잠시 생각했습니다. "제 생각에는, 제 어머니요."

page 38

하니 교장 선생님이 고개를 끄덕였습니다. "좋아, 프랜신. 양호실에 가서 기다리렴." 그는 다른 아이들을 바라보았습니다. "너희 나머지는 수업에 가야지."

잠시 후에, 프렌스키 부인이 프랜신을 데리러 왔습니다. 그들이 떠나는 동안에, 다른 아이들은 교실 창문으로 내다보고 있었습니다.

"너희는 프랜신의 이야기에 좀 수상한 구석이 있다고 생각하지 않았니?" 아서가 물었습니다.

"수상하다고?" 수 엘렌이 말했습니다. "나는 프랜신이 엄청나게 위험한 상황에서 살아남은 것 같은데."

"맞아." 버스터가 말했습니다. "하지만 내 말을 들어봐, 이야기의 앞뒤가 맞지 않아. 그러니까, 프렌신은 정말로 우리더러 그녀가 자신의 집안일을 하려고 급하게 집에 갔다는 걸 믿어주길 기대하는 거야? 그녀는 우리가 얼마나 멍청하다고 생각하는 거야?"

"내 생각엔 아서가 그 부분에 대해 이야기하는 게 아닌 거 같은데." 머피가 말했습니다. "내 생각에는 그는 자전거를—먹는 트럭을 말하는 거 같아."

"좋아." 랫번 선생님이 말했습니다. "다시 수업을 시작하자."

page 39

"흐으음." 브레인이 말했습니다. "그런 트럭이 정말로 있을 것 같진 않아. 누가 진짜로 자전거를 가져갔는지 우리가 알지 못하게 하려고 그녀가 그 부분을 지어냈을 수도 있을까?"

"왜 그녀가 그러겠어?" 머피가 물었습니다. "그것을 누가 가져갔던 간에 벌을 받아야 하지 않겠어?"

"어쩌면...." 버스터가 말했습니다. "그 도둑이 우리가 모두 아는 사람인 경우를 제외한다면 말이야."

다른 아이들이 눈을 크게 떴습니다. "네 말이 맞아." 아서가 말했습니다. "우리는 그건 생각하지 못했어."

7장

page 40

그날 밤 프렌스키 가족은 거실에 앉아서, TV를 보고 있었습니다.

"아빠." 프랜신이 말했습니다. "저 말씀 드릴 게 있어요."

"으-흠." 그녀의 아버지가 말했습니다. 그가 TV를 보고 있을 때, 가끔 그에게 말을 전달하는 건 어려웠습니다.

"제 자전거에 대한 거예요." 프랜신이 말을 이어갔습니다.

"네 자전거라고." 프렌스키 씨가 말을 반복했습니다.

프랜신은 깊게 숨을 들이마셨습니다. "그걸 도둑맞았어요." 그녀가 말했습니다. "거대한 갈고리가 달린 트럭이 있었고 저는 자전거에서 떨어졌고 저는 살아남은 게 다행이었어요."

page 41

"으-응." 그녀의 아버지가 말했습니다.

"세상에." 더 관심을 보이던, 그녀의 어머니가 말했습니다. "아슬아슬했구나. 정말 믿기 힘든 이야기야."

"너 진심으로 하는 소리야." 캐서린이 자신의 손톱을 칠하며 말했습니다.

프랜신은 자신의 의자에서 꼼지락거렸습니다.

"거대한 갈고리라고?" 그녀의 언니가 계속 말했습니다. "너 무슨 슈퍼 스파이 영화라도 찍고 있었니?"

"언니라고 다 아는 게 아니잖아!" 프랜신이 말했습니다. "그리고 언니는 거기에 없었다고."

"그만하렴, 캐서린." 프렌스키 부인이 말했습니다. "프랜신은 힘든 하루를 보냈단다. 그녀는 학교에서 몸이 안 좋아졌지..."

"그렇게 심하게는 아니죠." 캐서린이 말했습니다. "그녀가 토하거나 그런 건 아니잖아요."

"그렇다 해도, 넌 지금 도움이 안 돼. 네 손톱에나 집중하렴. 난 네가 한 곳을 칠하지 못한 것 같구나."

"어디요?" 캐서린이 물으면서, 자신의 손톱 하나하나를 미친 듯이 살펴보았습니다.

page 43

프랜신은 깊은 한숨을 내쉬었습니다. "그러니까 아빠는 화가 나지 않은 거죠, 아빠?"

그녀의 아버지는 눈을 깜빡였습니다. "화가 나? 뭐에 대해서?"

"제 도둑맞은 자전거에 대해서요."

프렌스키 씨는 뭐라고 말하려는 듯했지만, 그때 그는 자신의 아내가 짓는 표정을 알아챘습니다.

"난 기분이 좋다고는 말할 수 없겠구나, 프랜신." 그가 잠시 후에 말했습니다. "그 자전거는 내게 많은 추억이 있는 것이거든. 하지만 누군가가 네 자전거를 훔쳤다고 생각하는 건, 또한, 너에게도 힘든 일일 거야. 하지만 희망을 잃지 말렴. 어쩌면 그게 어떻게 해서든지 우리에게 돌아오게 될지도 모르니까."

캐서린은 자신의 눈을 굴렸습니다. "아빠, 그거는 자전거예요, 강아지가 아니라고요. 어쨌든, 제 생각에는 이 방에 있는 누군가는 그녀가 말하는 것보다 더 많이 알고 있는 것 같네요."

프랜신은 재빨리 일어났습니다. "전 자러 갈게요." 그녀가 말했습니다. "제가 나아지려면 더 많은 휴식이 필요해요."

page 44

그녀는 자신의 부모님에게 각각 잘 자라는 인사로 키스를 했고, 자신의 언니에게 혀를 삐죽 내밀고는, 방을 떠났습니다.

프랜신이 양치질을 하면서, 거울을 들여다보았습니다. 그녀는 캐서린이 그녀의 뒤에 있는 계단을 올라오는 것을 보았습니다.

"네 혀를 내미는 게 네 기분을 더 나아지게 해줄 순 있겠지." 캐서린이 말했습니다. "하지만 그건 아무것도 바꿔주지 않아. 나는 무슨 일이 있었는지 더 듣고 싶어. 넌 곧바로 경찰에게 갔니?"

"난 그러려고 했어." 프랜신이 대답했습니다. "하지만... 하지만 나는, 아, 내가 자전거에서 떨어졌을 때 머리를 부딪쳤고 기억상실증에 걸려버렸어. 내 기억이 되돌아왔을 때에는, 누군가를 잡기엔 너무 늦은 뒤였지."

"그건 우리가 저번 주에 봤던 영화에 나왔던 거잖아." 캐서린이 말했습니다. "네가 새 자전거를 갖고 싶다면 넌 그것보단 더 잘해야 할 거야."

프랜신은 더는 듣고 싶지 않았습니다. 그녀는 굳게 화장실 문을 닫았습니다.

"저리 가!" 그녀가 명령했습니다.

page 45

그녀는 씻는 것을 마쳤고 곧바로 잠자리에 들었습니다. 오랫동안 그녀는 천장을 쳐다보며, 금방이라도 거대한 갈고리가 천장을 뚫고 나와서 그녀를 잡아가는 상상을 했습니다. 하지만 그런 일은 전혀 없었고, 마침내 그녀는 잠이 들었습니다.

8장

page 46

프랜신이 다음 날 아침에 학교로 걸어가고 있을 때, 버스터와 머피가 그들의 자전거를 타고서 그녀를 만났습니다.

"우리에게 소식이 있어!" 버스터가 말했습니다. "엄청난 소식 말이야!"

"뭐에 대해서?" 프랜신이 물었습니다.

"세기의 범죄에 대해서지!" 버스터가 말했습니다.

"버스터가 말하려고 하는 건." 머피가 말했습니다. "바로 우리가 네 자전거에 무슨 일이 일어났는지 알고 있다는 거야."

프랜신은 얼굴을 찌푸렸습니다. "하지만 내가 이미 너희에게 무슨 일이 있었는지 말해줬잖아. 트럭이 있었고, 그리고—"

머피는 그녀의 손을 들어 올렸습니다. "좋은 시도야, 프랜신, 하지만 넌 우리를 속일 수 없어."

page 47

"그래?"

"프랜신, 우리는 네 친구야. 우리는 네가 진실을 말하고 있는지 분별할 수 있다고."

"그럴 수가 있다고?"

버스터가 고개를 끄덕였습니다. "물론이지. 그래서 네가 그 트럭 이야기를 지어냈다는 것을 우리가 알아챈 거야. 그리고 우리는 심지어 왜 그런지도 알지."

프랜신은 약간 어지러움을 느끼기 시작했습니다. "너희가 안다고?"

"왜냐하면 네가 누군가를 보호하려고 하기 때문이야." 머피가 말했습니다.

버스터는 그림 하나를 꺼내 프랜신에게 보여주었습니다.

"너의 자전거를 빼앗은 사람들, 그들 가운데 한 사람이 이렇게 생기지 않았니?"

"버스터, 저건 빙키처럼 생겼잖아."

"우리도 알아." 버스터가 말했습니다.

"빙키가 아니었어." 프랜신이 말했습니다.

"하지만 그럴 수밖에 없어." 버스터가 말했습니다. "자전거 전체를 훔칠 만큼 덩치가 큰 애가 또 누가 있니?"

page 48

"관두자." 프랜신이 말했습니다. "너희는 그냥 그것에 대해서 잊어버릴 수는 없니? 그건 네가 상관할 바가 아니잖아, 어차피."

머피는 상처받은 듯이 보였습니다. "우리는 그저 도우려고 했던 것뿐이야." 그녀가 말했습니다.

"뭐, 그러지마." 프랜신이 그녀에게 말했습니다. "그냥 나를 혼자 내버려둬."

그녀는 머피와 버스터를 그녀의 뒤에 남겨둔 채, 걸어가 버렸습니다.

"넌 어떻게 생각하니?" 버스터가 물었습니다.

"난 그녀가 아주 용감하게 굴고 있다고 생각해." 머피가 말했습니다. "하지만 부당한 일이 행해졌어. 그리고 우리는 이것을 바로 잡아야만 해."

잠시 뒤, 머피는 여러 아이들의 앞에 서 있었습니다. 그녀는 버스터의 그림을 흔들고 있었습니다.

"난 배후에 빙키가 있다고 생각해." 그녀가 아이들에게 말했습니다. "그리고 우리는 그가 자백하게 해야만 해."

page 49

"어떻게?" 브레인이 물었습니다.

"우리는 그를 협박할 수도 있어." 머피가 말했습니다. "자원할 사람?"

아무도 대답하지 않았습니다. 그들이 어떻게 빙키를 협박할 수 있겠어요? 그는 학급에서 가장 덩치가 큰 아이였습니다.

"너희는 정말 다 아기처럼 굴고 있어." 머피는 계속 말을 이어갔습니다. 그녀는 빙키가 그녀 뒤에서 걸어오고 있다는 걸 알아채지 못했습니다.

"음, 머피!" 아서가 말했습니다.

"방해하지 마. 내 가장 친하고 진정한 친구가 엄청난 충격을 받았다고." 그녀가 약간 훌쩍이며, 계속 말했습니다. "이러한 행위를 처벌하지 않고 그냥 둘

수는 없어. 그리고 만약 크로스와이어 혼자서 이런 악덕한 불의와 싸워야 한다면, 좋아. 그것은 처음도 아니고, 또 그건—"

"야!" 빙키가 외쳤습니다.

머피는 뒤돌아섰습니다.

빙키가 그녀를 쏘아보았습니다. "넌 내가 프랜신의 자전거를 훔쳤다고 모두에게 말하고 있는 거야?"

"그렇다면? 그거에 죄책감을 느끼니?"

page 51

"아니. 왜냐하면 난 그걸 훔치지 않았거든."

"그렇다면 누가 그랬겠어?" 머피가 따졌습니다. "더 좋은 생각이라도 있니?"

빙키는 어깨를 으쓱거렸고 자신의 고개를 저었습니다. "아니, 나는 그저 내가 한 게 아니라는 것만 알아."

"그만해!"

프랜신은 아이들의 뒤에서 소리치고 있었습니다. "빙키를 그만 괴롭혀. 걔는 아무것도 안 했어."

빙키가 투덜거렸습니다. "내가 말했듯이 말이야."

"그렇다면 네 자전거에는 무슨 일이 있었던 거야?" 머피가 물었습니다.

"그것은... 그건 실수로 쓰레기들과 함께 수거되어 버렸어." 프랜신이 조용히 말했습니다.

머피가 그림을 떨어뜨렸습니다.

"프랜신!" 그녀가 외쳤습니다. "왜 우리에게 말해주지 않은 거야?"

프랜신은 어떻게 말해야 할지 몰랐습니다.

"미안해, 빙키." 머피가 말했습니다. "넌 나를 용서해줄 수 있겠니?"

page 52

"그리고 나도 미안해." 버스터가 말했습니다.

빙키는 어깨를 으쓱했습니다. "그럼." 그가 말했습니다. "나는 강인한 사람이잖아, 알지?"

그러더니 그는 걸어가 버렸습니다.

머피는 바닥에 주저앉았습니다. "갑자기, 나는 기분이 별로 좋지 않아."

프랜신은 고개를 끄덕였습니다. "나와 같은 신세네." 그녀가 말했습니다.

9장

page 53

해가 지고 있을 때 프랜신과 그녀의 아버지는 쓰레기장으로 출발했습니다. 프랜신은 경찰을 따돌리기 위해 도둑들이 그녀의 자전거를 거기에 버렸다고 그녀의 아버지에게 말하고 싶었습니다. 하지만, 그녀가 캐서린에게 그 이야기를 시험 삼아 말했을 때, 그녀의 언니는 웃음을 멈추지 못했습니다.

"그건 너무 우스꽝스럽잖아." 캐서린이 그녀에게 말했습니다. "아무리 너라고 해도 말이야."

결국 프랜신은 직장에 있는 그녀의 아버지에게 전화했고 그에게 진실을 말했습니다.

"아빠, 도둑들이 그런 게 아니었어요." 그녀는 전화로 그에게 말했습니다. "그건 사고였어요."

page 54

"그렇구나." 그녀의 아버지가 조용히 대답했습니다.

"정말 아빠가 엄밀히 따지려고 한다면, 그게 제 잘못이라고 할 수는 있죠."

"난 네가 그렇다고 인정하는 걸 듣게 되어서 기쁘구나."

"그래요?" 프랜신은 놀랐습니다. "아빠는 이미 알고 계셨다는 거예요? 하지만 아무 말도 하지 않으셨잖아요?"

"왜냐하면 난 네가 먼저 말해주길 바랐으니까."

"오."

"그리고 난 네가 말해줘서 자랑스럽단다. 물론, 난 네가 왜 그랬는지 설명해주길 바라고 있지만 말이야."

"왜냐하면 모든 사람이 저를 놀렸기 때문이에요. 하지만 저는 자전거를 버리려고 했던 것이 아니었어요. 저는 잠시 그걸 숨겨두려던 거였어요. 그러고 나서 쓰레기 트럭이 그것을 수거했을 때, 저는 그게 제 문제를 해결해줄 수도 있다고 생각했어요."

"그래서 그렇게 됐니?"

프랜신은 고개를 저었습니다. "아니요. 상황은 단지 점점 더 악화되었어요."

page 55

"난 네가 어떻게 느꼈을지 이해할 수 있단다. 하지만 그것에 대해 거짓말을 하는 것에는 변명의 여지가 없어."

"알아요, 아빠. 저는 아빠의 기분을 상하게 하고 싶지 않았던 것 같아요. 저는 그 자전거가 아빠에게 얼마나 큰 의미가 있는지 알고 있었어요. 정말 죄송해요. 이제 우리 어떻게 해야 해요?"

"우린 쓰레기장으로 갈 거란다." 프렌스키씨가 전화로 말했습니다.

그리고 이제 그들이 여기에 왔습니다. 프렌스키 씨는 경비원에게 질문을 했고, 그는 그들에게 막 수거한 쓰레기가 있는 곳을 알려줬습니다.

"이제 어떡해요?" 프랜신이 물었습니다.

"우리는 찾으러 가야지." 그녀의 아버지가 말했습니다.

"아빠는 그러니까 우리가 해야만—"

그녀의 아버지가 고개를 끄덕였습니다. "이게 네 벌의 일부라고 생각하렴, 아가씨. 적어도 자전거는 눈에 띌 만큼 크긴 하잖니."

프랜신은 막대기로 쓰레기를 뒤지기 시작했습니다. 거기에는 옆으로 밀쳐내야 할 오래된 피자 상자와 바나나 껍질 그리고 부서진 장난감들이 있었습니다.

page 56

냄새는 끔찍했습니다. 프랜신은 자신의 숨을 참으려고 했지만, 잘 되지 않았습니다. 그녀는 자기 코를 잡고는 가능한 숨을 적게 들이마시려고 했습니다.

"전 기절할 것 같아요." 그녀가 말했습니다.

"만약 그렇게 한다면." 그녀의 아버지가 말했습니다. "네가 어떤 것 위로 쓰러질지 누가 알겠니."

"좋은 지적이네요." 프랜신이 말했습니다. 아마 기절하는 건 그리 좋은 생각이 아닌 것 같았습니다.

"아하!" 프렌스키 씨가 말했습니다. 그는 허리를 숙여 구겨진 종이와 컵들을 밀쳐냈습니다. "이것 봐, 여기 있네!"

그는 자전거를 들어올려 꺼냈습니다.

프랜신이 생각하기에, 오래된 자전거의 한 가지 좋은 점은 그것이 하룻밤 동안 쓰레기장에 있었어도 딱히 더 나빠 보이지 않는다는 것이었습니다.

"아빠는 정말 그걸 타고 매일 학교에 가셨어요?" 그녀가 물었습니다.

그녀의 아버지가 미소 지었습니다. "왕복으로 오르막길이었지."

프랜신은 새로운 경외심을 가지고 그 자전거를 바라보았습니다. "와. 있잖아요, 어쩌면 우리가 이걸 고칠 수 있을지도 몰라요."

page 58

그녀의 아버지는 어깨를 으쓱했습니다. 그는 헝겊을 꺼내서 자전거를 닦기 시작했습니다.

"어때요, 아빠? 그것이 정말로 필요한 건 단지 새로운 페인트칠이에요."

프렌스키 씨가 프랜신을 보았습니다. "글쎄..." 그는 크게 미소 지었습니다. "우리가 망설일 것이 뭐가 있겠니?"

10장

page 59

프렌스키 가족의 아파트 밖에서, 가족 전체가 서서 기다리고 있었습니다.

"왜 *제가* 여기에 있어야 하죠?" 캐서린이 물었습니다.

"넌 가족의 일원이잖니." 그녀의 어머니가 말했습니다. "그리고 이건 가족이 함께하는 순간이고."

"엄마가 그렇게 말씀하실까 봐 두려웠어요." 캐서린이 중얼거렸습니다.

그들 앞에서는, 하얀 침대 시트가 낡은 자전거 위에 씌워져 있었는데, 그것은 프랜신과 그녀의 아버지가 일주일 동안 작업해온 것이었습니다.

"좋지 않기만 해봐." 캐서린이 말했습니다.

page 60

"숙녀 여러분 그리고... 숙녀 여러분." 프렌스키 씨가 둘러보며, 말했습니다. "소개합니다, 프랜신의 새롭고 개선되었으며, 완전히 복구된..."

그가 시트를 벗겼습니다.

"... 자전거를!"

프랜신과 그녀의 어머니가 박수를 쳤습니다.

그 새로운 자전거는 밝게 페인트칠이 되어 있었습니다. 그것은 여전히 보라색이었지만, 이제는 별처럼 반짝였습니다. 그리고 바나나 모양의 안장은 문질러지고 닦여져, 오래된 비닐에 광택이 다시 살아났습니다.

"아름답네요!" 프렌스키 부인이 말했습니다. "올리버, 당신과 프랜신이 정말 멋지게 해내었어요."

프랜신이 활짝 웃었습니다.

"감사해요, 감사합니다." 그녀의 아버지가 말했습니다. "고백하건대 마무리로, 펜더에 경주용 줄무늬를 넣는 것은 프랜신의 생각이었어."

page 61

"다른 누구도 그런 것은 갖고 있지 않아요." 프랜신이 말했습니다. "심지어 머피에게도 없어요."

"난 색이 마음에 들어." 캐서린이 인정했습니다. "사실은." 그녀가 덧붙이며, 자신의 손을 내밀었습니다, "내 손톱에 바르면 예쁘겠어."

"흠, 프랜신." 그녀의 아버지가 말했습니다. "저보다 더 나은 칭찬은 없겠구나." 그는 잠시 말을 멈추었습니다. "그리고 이제 진실의 순간이란다—시범 주행을 해야지. 프랜신, 네가 그 영광을 누려보겠니?"

그는 허리를 숙여 인사했고 옆으로 물러섰습니다. 하지만 프랜신은 자신의 헬멧을 내밀었습니다.

"먼저 해보세요, 아빠."

"정말이니? 난 네 중요한 순간을 빼앗고 싶지는 않은데."

프랜신은 미소 지었습니다. "정말이에요."

프렌스키 씨는 프랜신의 헬멧을 받아 들었고 그것을 채워서 썼습니다.

"조심해요, 여보!" 프렌스키 부인이 말했습니다.

page 63

그는 그녀의 걱정을 일축했습니다. "걱정하지 마, 여보. 자전거를 타는 건 마치, 그러니까, 자전거를 타는 법과 같지. 어떻게 하는지 절대 잊지 않는다고."

"아마 그렇겠죠." 캐서린이 말했습니다, "하지만 아무한테도 들키지 마세요, 제발요."

"최선을 다하도록 하마. 저 블록 주위를 조금 돌고 올게. 난 이게 완전히 안전한지 확인하고 싶을 뿐이야."

그는 자전거에 올라탔고 보도를 따라서 비틀거리며 갔습니다. 그가 모퉁이를 돌았을 때, 그는 멈춰서 자신이 시야 밖에 있는 것을 확인했습니다. 그러더니 그는 빠르게 멀어져 갔고 길을 따라 쌩하고 달리면서, 그의 얼굴이 즐거움으로 환해졌습니다.

"그가 괜찮을 거 같아?" 그녀의 아버지가 시야에서 사라지자 캐서린이 물었습니다.

"물론이지." 프랜신이 말했습니다. 만약 이 모든 경험이 그녀에게 가르쳐준 것이 있다면, 그것은 그녀가 언제나 자신의 아버지를 믿을 수 있다는 것이었습니다.

Chapter 1

1. B The Frenskys were eating dinner in their apartment. At least Mr. and Mrs. Frensky and their older daughter, Catherine, were eating dinner. Their younger daughter, Francine, was not eating at all. She was just sitting in her chair with her arms folded.

2. D "It means you're a little, uh, out of sorts," said her father, Oliver. "A bit upset about not getting your way." "Well, why shouldn't I be?" said Francine. "I'm sorry, honey," said her mother, Laverne. "But we can't afford to get you a new bike right now. Maybe next year. . ."

3. A Francine continued to sulk. "It's not fair. I'll just *die* without a bike."

4. D Francine's face fell. This bike was not only old. It was also ugly. Bright purple with chipped paint, rusted handlebars, and a glittery burnt-orange banana seat. "What *is* it?" she asked. "Your new bike," her father explained. "Well, actually it's an old new bike." He wiped off an enormous cobweb between the handlebars. "Dad, bikes have changed a lot since the Stone Age." Her father inspected it. "I don't know about that. They still have two wheels, a seat, and handlebars. And you don't see a banana seat like this every day. Definitely a collector's item." "But I don't want a collector's item. I want a cross bike with twenty-one gears."

5. C Francine's face fell. This bike was not only old. It was also ugly.

Chapter 2

1. C "I never watch that show," said Muffy, locking up her bike. "There are much more educational and important things to watch." "Like what?" Buster and Arthur said together. "The Home Shopping Channel, of course. If you don't pay attention to that, you can miss some really fabulous buying opportunities."

2. A "I could have had any bike I wanted," said Francine. "But I chose this one." Muffy frowned. "But Francine . . . why?" "Um, tradition. This bike was my dad's. It's like a family heirloom. He was able to do all kinds of tricks with

it."

3. B "It is confusing," agreed Mr. Ratburn. "In this case I believe it was the Sumerians. Can anyone tell us what these ancient people might have done with their new wheel?" Buster waved his arm wildly. "Yes, Buster?" "Built Francine's bicycle."

4. C "Stop picking on Francine," Muffy told Buster. "Yeah!" said Francine. "It's not her fault she has to ride an ugly, old bicycle," Muffy went on. Francine blinked. "Oh?"

5. A Buster's face changed in mid-laugh. He looked embarrassed. So did everyone else. They got very quiet. But none of them felt as embarrassed as Francine did, deep down inside where nobody could see.

Chapter 3

1. D Well, even if no one had taken the bike, that didn't mean she had to keep looking at it. Glancing around, she noticed some bushes at the edge of the school yard. She wheeled the bike into them and rested it behind a garbage can.

2. A Arthur poked Buster in the side. "Buster has something he wants to say to you, don't you, Buster?" "Um, yes, I do," said Buster. He cleared his throat. "Francine, I'm sorry for what I said before. Insulting your bike, I mean."

3. B "And we're sorry we laughed, too," said Arthur. "You know, my father has a beat-up frying pan from his early cooking days. It's all black, with a few dents and scratches. I once asked him why he didn't buy a shiny new one to use instead. He said there was something friendly about the old pan that just made food taste better. I'm sure your bike was like that for your dad."

4. C "Where is your bike, anyway?" she asked. "Oh, um, I'm not using it right at the moment. . . . I just feel like walking."

5. A Francine wasn't really in the mood. Even though she was glad her friends had apologized, she still felt out of place. Why did she have to be the one to stand out? She didn't want people to feel sorry for her—even if they *were* nice

about it.

Chapter 4

1. C   With every bounce, Francine wished for another bike. And not just any bike. A bike that would make Arthur and Buster wish they had one, too. A bike even Muffy would admire.

2. A   "The bike is purple," Francine said dully. "Very purple." Her father nodded. "That was my favorite color when I was your age. Purple is the color of royalty, you know. Dignified. Majestic."

3. D   "So you won?" Her father laughed. "Not exactly. The bruiser won—as usual. But at least I was right in the middle. For me that was a big improvement."

4. D   Her father looked at her. "Don't look so disappointed, Francine. I was really happy just to do better."

5. B   Mr. Frensky sighed. "I wish I could get you a new one, honey. But we don't have the extra money right now. And my old bike has a long and proud history. I'm afraid that's going to have to satisfy you for now."

Chapter 5

1. B   The next morning, Francine walked slowly to school. She had hoped that the start of a new day would make her feel better. But even though the sun was shining and the birds were singing, she felt just as bad as she had the day before.

2. C   Just then, one of the men picked up Francine's bike and threw it into the truck. Francine started to run. "Hey! Hey!" she shouted, waving her arms. "Come back here! You've got my bike in there!"

3. A   Suddenly Francine had an idea. "My, um, bike was stolen," she explained. "Stolen!" said Arthur. "Are you sure?"

4. B   Muffy looked confused. "Why would anyone steal that—I mean, your bike?" She asked. Francine shrugged. "It *was* pretty old . . ." Muffy gasped.

"Hey, *that* could be the reason! What if it was so old it was an antique?" She started waving her arms. "Help! Police!"

5. A "No! Wait!" said Francine. She didn't want to drag the school principal into this. But it was too late. All the other kids were running into the school.

Chapter 6

1. A Francine thought for a moment. "Oh, you know, cleaning my room, helping to make dinner." "Wow, I'm impressed," the Brain whispered to Buster. "I never hurry home to do my chores." They were standing behind Francine with Arthur and Muffy.

2. C *Francine could see herself riding along on her bike, whistling happily. All of a sudden a big truck came up behind her. It was kind of like a garbage truck, but with a big claw on the back. The claw reached down and grabbed Francine's bike. She just managed to jump off before the claw lifted the bike up and dropped it into the truck.*

3. C "We need to put out an APB!" said Buster. "APB?" said Muffy. "All Points Bulletin," Arthur explained. Buster nodded. "The state police should blanket the highways. They should search every rest stop."

4. D Listening to Buster, Francine found herself feeling more and more uncomfortable. "Um, Mr. Haney . . . I know the day hasn't really started yet, but can I go home? I don't feel very well. "You do look a little pale," said Mr. Haney. "We'll have the nurse check you out. If she agrees, who should I call to come get you?"

5. B "Hmmm," said the Brain. "Such a truck does seem a little unlikely. Is it possible she invented that part to keep us from finding out who really took her bike?" "Why would she do that?" asked Muffy. "Shouldn't whoever took it be punished?" "Unless . . . ," said Buster. "Unless the thief is somebody *we all know.*

Chapter 7

1. A Francine took a deep breath. "It's been stolen," she said. "There was this

truck with a giant claw and I was knocked off and I'm lucky to be alive." "Uh-huh," said her father. "Goodness," said her mother, who was paying more attention. "What a close call. That sounds unbelievable."

2. D "You're not kidding," said Catherine as she painted her fingernails. Francine squirmed in her chair.

3. A "I can't say I'm happy, Francine," he said after a moment. "That bike held a lot of memories for me. But it must be hard for you, too, thinking about someone stealing your bike. But don't give up hope. Maybe it will find its way back to us somehow."

4. D "Sticking your tongue out may make you feel better," said Catherine, "but it doesn't change anything. I want to hear more about what happened. Did you go right to the police?" "I would have," Francine said back. "But . . . but I, ah, hit my head when I fell off my bike and got amnesia. By the time my memory came back, it was too late to catch anyone."

5. B "That's from the movie we saw last week," said Catherine. "You'll have to do better than that if you want a new bike."

Chapter 8

1. C We've got news!" said Buster. "Big news!" "About what?" Francine asked. "About the crime of the century!" said Buster. "What Buster is trying to say," said Muffy, "is that we think we know what happened to your bike."

2. D "The guys who swiped your bike, did one of them look like this?" "Buster, that looks like Binky." "We know," Buster said.

3. B "It wasn't Binky," said Francine. "But it has to be," said Buster. "Who else is big enough to steal a whole bike?"

4. A "I say Binky's behind it," she told the crowd. "And we have to make him confess." "How?" asked the Brain. "We could threaten him," said Muffy. "Any volunteers?" Nobody answered. How could they threaten Binky? He was the biggest kid in the class.

5. B "I'm sorry, Binky," said Muffy. "Can you ever forgive me?" "And me, too,"

said Buster. Binky shrugged. "Sure," he said. "I'm a tough guy, remember?" Then he walked away. Muffy sat down on the ground. "All of a sudden, I don't feel very good."

Chapter 9

1. A The sun was setting as Francine and her father started off for the dump. Francine had wanted to tell her father that the thieves had dropped her bike there to throw the police off their trail. However, when she had tried this story out on Catherine, her sister couldn't stop laughing.

2. B "I guess if you were really being technical, you could say it was my fault." "I'm glad to hear you admit it." "You are?" Francine had been surprised. "You mean you knew already? But you didn't say anything?" "Because I wanted you to say something first."

3. A "I can understand how you felt. But it's no excuse for lying about it." "I know, Dad. I guess I didn't want to hurt your feelings. I knew how much the bike meant to you. I'm really sorry. What do we do now?"

4. C Her father nodded. "Consider it part of your punishment, young lady. At least the bike is big enough to stand out." Francine started poking through the garbage with a stick. There were old pizza boxes and banana peels and broken toys to push aside.

5. A One good thing about an old bike, thought Francine, is that it can sit in the dump overnight and not look any worse. "Did you really ride that

Chapter 10

1. D Outside the Frenskys' apartment, the whole family was standing ready. "Why do I have to be here?" Catherine asked. "You're part of the family," said her mother. "And this is a family moment."

2. B In front of them, a white bed sheet had been draped over the old bike, which Francine and her father had been working on for a week.

3. C The new bike was brightly painted. It was still purple, but now it gleamed

like a star. And the banana seat had been rubbed and polished, restoring the luster to the old vinyl. "Beautiful!" said Mrs. Frensky. "Oliver, you and Francine did a wonderful job." Francine beamed. "Thank you, thank you," said her father. "I have to confess that the finishing touch, the racing stripes on the fenders, were Francine's idea."

4. D "And now the moment of truth—the test drive. Francine, will you do the honors?" He bowed and stepped aside. But Francine held out her helmet. "You first, Dad." "Are you sure? I wouldn't want to deprive you of your big moment."

5. C He mounted the bike and wobbled down the sidewalk. As he rounded the corner, he stopped to make sure he was out of sight. Then he pushed off fast and whizzed down the street, his face lit up with glee.

아서와 도둑맞은 자전거의 미스터리
(Arthur and the Mystery of the Stolen Bike)

1판 1쇄   2016년 1월 4일
1판 7쇄   2020년 8월 7일

지은이 Marc Brown
기획 이수영
책임편집 정소이 김보경
콘텐츠제작및감수 롱테일북스 편집부
저작권 김보경
마케팅 김보미 정경훈

펴낸이 이수영
펴낸곳 (주)롱테일북스
출판등록 제2015-000191호
주소 04043 서울특별시 마포구 양화로 12길 16-9(서교동) 북앤빌딩 3층
전자메일 helper@longtailbooks.co.kr
(학원 · 학교에서 본도서를 교재로 사용하길 원하시는 경우 전자메일로 문의주시면
자세한 안내를 받으실 수 있습니다.)

ISBN 979-11-86701-04-1 14740

롱테일북스는 (주)북하우스 퍼블리셔스의 계열사입니다.

이 도서의 국립중앙도서관 출판시도서목록(CIP)은 서지정보유통지원시스템 홈페이지(http://seoji.nl.go.kr)와
국가자료공동목록시스템(http://www.nl.go.kr/kolisnet)에서 이용하실 수 있습니다. (CIP 제어번호 : CIP2015030891)